THE
WATERGATE
QUIZ BOOK

☆☆☆ |THE| ☆☆☆

WATERGATE

QUIZ BOOK

W. S. Moorhead

A NEW REPUBLIC BOOK

HOLT, RINEHART AND WINSTON | NEW YORK

Special thanks to Erica for her support,
and to Marc, Felicia, Jim, J.L., and the Ability Group

Copyright © 1983 by W. S. Moorhead
All rights reserved, including the right to reproduce
this book or portions thereof in any form.
Published by Holt, Rinehart and Winston,
383 Madison Avenue, New York, New York 10017.
Published simultaneously in Canada by Holt, Rinehart
and Winston of Canada, Limited.

Library of Congress Cataloging in Publication Data
Moorhead, W. S.
The Watergate quiz book.
"A New republic book."
1. Watergate Affair, 1972– —Miscellanea.
I. Title.
E860.M66   1983   364.1′32′0973   83-34
ISBN: 0-03-063534-9

First Edition

Designer: Victoria Hartman
Printed in the United States of America
1   3   5   7   9   10   8   6   4   2

Photos 1–6, taken by the author, are from exhibits
at the burglars' trial; all other photos
are from the Nixon Project archives.

To my sister Penny, Dad, and
The Friends of Bill Moorhead

"After the history of the first term is written and you look back, you're going to see that, compared to other administrations or by any other standards you'd want to apply, that it has been an extraordinarily clean, corruption-free administration, because the President insists on that."
—*John Ehrlichman, September 7, 1972*

"Watch what we do, not what we say."
—*John Mitchell*

Contents

INTRODUCTION

Ten years ago the greatest scandal in American political history was coming to light. Some of us drank it in daily, savoring every new revelation or outrage. Some of us tried to follow the goings-on, but never sorted out the details. And some of us, finally worn down by the numberless charges, countercharges, and innuendoes, and mystified by interlocking bureaucratic chains of command, did our best to ignore the whole thing (all the while suspecting that everyone involved was probably guilty of something).

The Watergate Quiz Book is for you whether you thought Watergate was a national joke or a national disgrace, whether you sat in front of the tube and screamed "Guilty, guilty, guilty" as one TV witness after another grinned and lied, or didn't watch at all. The book is a delicious opportunity for buffs to wallow anew in Watergate, and also an irreverent and ironic chronicle for anyone who missed (or avoided) many of Watergate's "bombshells."

Watergate is undeniably the greatest political scandal in our history, but it is also one of the century's greatest entertainments, starring a man who held America's highest political office, was proven to have deliberately lied to the public for more than two years, but when finally hounded out of office still had the nerve to say, "I wasn't lying. I said things that later on seemed to be untrue."

Return with me now to those thrilling days of wiretapping, spies, tough guys, coded memoranda and code names, paper-shredding extravaganzas, government burglaries, interagency sabotage, big-dollar influence peddling, international financial schemes, and an epic showdown among the three branches of government. Welcome back effrontery, sheer gall, bald-faced lies, paranoia in high places, "inoperative" information, and vaulting ambition o'erleaping itself! Remember the "Rose Mary Stretch"? Did you know which presidential aides were *not*

1

recruited from the J. Walter Thompson advertising agency's Los Angeles office? Did you ever learn what "Gemstone" was? Operation Candor? The Mullen Agency? What did the President know, and when did he know it?

The Watergate Quiz Book organizes two years of confusing allegations, revelations, and testimony into ten chronological chapters of nasty and challenging questions—true/false, multiple choice, direct response, and—for Watergate fanatics only—"Deep Throat" questions.

Test your Watergate IQ—or learn it all for the first time.

W. S. Moorhead
Washington, D.C.

☆ 1 ☆

THE PLUMBERS

"It's hard to explain. It's a constant barrage. . . . Henry [Kissinger] and others go around wringing their hands for the President. . . . After a while you lose your perspective. . . . All of the things that you think about later you become inured to while in the White House. It isn't a matter of constant moral torment when you're there."   —*Roger Morris, White House aide*

"What those fellows [the Plumbers] did was no crime; they ought to get a medal for going after Ellsberg."
          —*President Nixon, April 18, 1973*

THE TIMES *(1969–1972)*

The Vietnam War rancored the American political scene increasingly as it became clear that the new Administration was unable to deliver a tidy conclusion to the conflict. The White House could not keep sensitive internal information from surfacing in the press, and increasingly saw itself as persecuted by antiwar left-wingers and black militants.

Quickly slipping into a siege mentality, the White House developed a ravenous appetite for covert intelligence. The demonstrations, random acts of violence, and lawlessness of antiwar activists seemed to Nixon to justify the sort of rough, gutter warfare usually relegated only to the world of professional agents in the international struggle against Soviet-backed communism. As existing U.S. government agencies were unable or unwilling to cooperate, Nixon began chartering his own spies ("the Plumbers") in secret.

Right after the 1968 election, Nixon started wiretapping White House aides and newsmen. At Nixon's insistence, aide Tom Huston drew up plans for a sweeping scheme of internal espionage, complete with "black bag" jobs and sabotage. When former Pentagon official Daniel Ellsberg gave classified documents (the Pentagon Papers) to *The New York Times*, the White House hounded him viciously.

QUESTIONS

1. To what was Attorney General Kleindienst referring when he said "that zoo up the street"?

2. Certain White House aides may have thought that they were above the law, but none ever stated so publicly. True or false?

3. About whom was White House director of communications Ken Clawson speaking when he said the following: "There is no policy [he] is responsible for, yet there is no policy he doesn't have a hand in somehow"?
   a) Haldeman
   b) Colson
   c) Dean

4. In the following, is Haldeman describing Ehrlichman or is Ehrlichman describing Haldeman: ". . . my crafty friend who loved intrigue and was given [to] the more devious approach"?

5. What man—an expert on the esoteric legal points of municipal-bond financing, recognized as without peer in this legal specialty by 1967—allowed Nixon to join his profitable practice, and in less than six years had ruined his family life, nearly lost his wife, watched his law practice dissipate, was no longer speaking to the President, faced multiple indictments on a host of criminal charges, and finally went to jail?

6. What key Nixon advisor disavowed participation in White House wiretapping and knowledge of the Plumbers, and, by cultivating his public image as the one solid higher-up in the besieged White House, managed to avoid serious investigation by Watergate prosecutors and the Senate Watergate Committee?

7. What member of the Nixon Administration had the following nicknames: The Cold Bastard, Chief of Dirty Tricks, King of the Hardhats, Mr. Dirty Tricks, Hatchet Man, Superloyalist, The Power Mechanic, and Chief Ass Kicker?

8. What man saw his legal stature rise, his practice grow to include clients like Atlantic-Richfield and United Air Lines, became Nixon's personal attorney (preparing even his tax returns and residential purchase documents), raised money for Nixon's campaigns, ran the enormous post-1968 campaign surplus as a slush fund to finance dirty tricks, acted as bagman for hush money to silence Watergate burglars, and finally went to jail?

9. What member of the Administration had the following nicknames: Iron Butt, Nicks, Gloomy Gus, The Mad Monk, Le Grande Fromage, Thelma's Husband, and Rufus?

10. What was Bebe Rebozo's nickname for Nixon?

11. What man refused a full scholarship to Harvard because he was "turned off at the bomb-throwers in Harvard Square," played a marginal role in the 1968 campaign, yet in one year under Halde-

man's sponsorship became the focal point for White House "dirty tricks," and, before pleading guilty to obstruction of justice, became a born-again Christian?

12. What member of the Administration had these nicknames: Mr. Inside, The Prussian, Lord High Executioner, Nixon's SOB, and Chief Frog Man?

13. What man, a personal friend of Nixon's for twenty-seven years, and the director of communications for the Executive Branch for five years, did Nixon praise lavishly in public while privately saying to Haldeman, "You've just not got to let _____ ever set up a meeting again. . . . He just opens it up and sits there with eggs on his face. . . . He just doesn't have his head screwed on, Bob. . . . He just sort of blubbers around."

14. What member of the Administration was variously nicknamed The Pipe, The Big Enchilada, and Old Stone Face?

15. What pair of Nixon Administration individuals had the following nicknames: Berlin Wall, Katzenjammer Kids, German Shepherds, Nazis, and Hans & Fritz?

16. Which of the following members of the Administration was *not* a lawyer?
    a) Nixon
    b) Haldeman
    c) Ehrlichman
    d) Mardian
    e) Mitchell
    f) Kleindienst
    g) Young
    h) Dean
    i) Colson
    j) Agnew
    k) Kalmbach
    l) Krogh
    m) Liddy
    n) Strachan

17. Which one of the following presidential aides was *not* recruited from the Los Angeles office of the J. Walter Thompson advertising agency?
    a) Haldeman
    b) Chapin
    c) Ziegler
    d) Dean
    e) Higby

18. Which of the following advertising accounts did Haldeman *not* manage for J. Walter Thompson?
    a) Sani-Flush
    b) Airwick
    c) Black Flag

19. What was Jeb Magruder's profession when he was first approached about working in the Nixon White House?
    a) Securities litigator with Webster & Sheffield in New York
    b) Management consultant with Strategic Planning Associates in Washington
    c) Buyer of women's accessories for the Broadway Department Store in Los Angeles

20. Nixon's press secretary, Ron Ziegler, once worked as a tour guide on the "Jungle Ride" at Disneyland. True or false?

21. What principle did Colson tell White House aides served to guide him throughout his public-service career?
    a) "Public access to government documents is essential to the successful operation of a democracy."
    b) "When you've got them by the balls, their hearts and minds will follow."
    c) "With malice toward none and charity for all."

22. What was the average age of the following members of the Nixon Administration at the time of their appointments: John Dean, Fred Fielding, Egil Krogh, Gordon Strachan, Bruce Kehrli, Hugh Sloan, Robert Odle, Robert Reisner, and Dwight Chapin?
    a) 35–38
    b) 32–35
    c) Under 30

23. Who said about Colson, "He says hop and you hop"?
    a) Nixon
    b) Colson's wife
    c) Rose Mary Woods

24. What pair of individuals were nicknamed "Colson's Gunners"?

25. Who termed Colson "viciously loyal"?
    a) Nixon
    b) Colson
    c) Colson's father

26. What was the "tickler"?

27. Which of the following films was *not* shown in the White House by Nixon aides during the Nixon Administration?
    a) The "Checkers speech"
    b) Pornographic movies
    c) Nazi propaganda films

28. What was presidential "deniability"?

29. What did Deep Throat call the willingness of the President's aides to fight dirty for keeps regardless of how such behavior might harm the country?
    a) "Sanctimonious thuggery"
    b) "Switchblade mentality"
    c) "Guttersniping"

30. Despite sensationalistic publicity, there never was a formal, written "enemies list." True or false?

31. Given that the White House had a plan to "screw" political enemies by using various government agencies, what was the name of the plan it had to reward friends?
    a) "Incumbency-Responsiveness Program"
    b) "Friends of Richard Nixon"
    c) "Checkers' Mates"

32. What did Dean find to be an "exciting prospect" in his famous meeting with Nixon on September 15, 1972?
    a) Nixon's beating McGovern in the November election
    b) Keeping tabs on the Administration's enemies and getting them after the election
    c) Dean's being made one of the Plumbers

33. What peculiar Watergate-related tie bound Paul Newman, Mary McGrory, Allard Lowenstein, and Leonard Woodcock?

34. Why did Dean suggest to Nixon that the IRS would resist being used by Nixon to attack his political enemies?
    a) There were too many Democrats in the agency.
    b) Negative consequences might result from possible illegality.
    c) The bureaucrats would be afraid of being fired when the Democrats came back in power.

35. To whom was Nixon referring when he said the following? "He didn't get Secretary of Treasury because he has nice blue eyes. It was a goddamn favor to him to get that job. . . . If he doesn't do it [i.e., let the IRS be used for political purposes], he is out as Secretary of Treasury, and that is the way it is going to be played."

36. Whom did Magruder assign to disrupt an antiwar, anti-Hoover demonstration outside the Capitol on May 4, 1972?

37. What souvenir did Colson want Liddy to bring to Nixon from the demonstration?
    a) A "Jail to the Chief" poster
    b) A Vietcong flag
    c) A "Peace with Honor" button

38. Colson suggested to Nixon that some "thugs" be rounded up to break up demonstrations. Where did Colson expect to get thugs?
    a) Anti-Castro Cuban exiles
    b) The Teamsters Union
    c) "Hardhats for Nixon"

39. Colson recruited Watergate burglars Barker and Sturgis to show up uninvited at Cuban exile meetings in May 1972 for what purpose?
    a) To recruit more Plumbers
    b) To turn the meetings into pro-Nixon rallies
    c) To recruit helpers to launder money

40. In addition to participating in the Watergate burglary, the Cubans were also paid to create riots, even to urinate and defecate in public. True or false?

41. Who was Richard M. Dixon, and did the White House really care?

42. Nixon approved the Huston plan, which contained provisions for government-sponsored illegal entry, mail openings, etc., to combat radical elements in American society. True or false?

43. The White House successfully implemented the "Huston plan." True or false?

44. Was the Huston plan formally canceled by Nixon?

45. Tom Huston did not regard as illegal that part of his plan which called for surreptitious entry and other such procedures for gathering domestic intelligence. True or false?

46. What congressman put the entire details of the Huston plan into the *Congressional Record*?
    a) Rep. William S. Moorhead
    b) Rep. Carlos Moorhead
    c) Rep. Philip Crane

47. In 1970, what U.S. government agency concluded that there was "no substantial evidence to support the Nixon Administration's view that foreign governments were supplying undercover agents and funds to radicals and Black Panther groups in the U.S.," thus directly contradicting an underlying justification for the Huston plan?
    a) CIA
    b) FBI
    c) NSC

48. Why was the White House "non-legal internal investigations unit" nicknamed the Plumbers?

49. Which one of the following was *not* a Plumber?
    a) Young
    b) Colson
    c) Krogh
    d) Hunt
    e) Liddy

50. Hunt testified before the Senate Watergate Committee that during his twenty-one years with the CIA, he "was trained in the

techniques of physical and electronic surveillance, photography, document forgery, and surreptitious entries into guarded premises for photography and installation of electronic devices. I participated in and had the responsibility for a number of such entries. . . ." Despite his qualifications, Hunt told the committee that he was hired to perform entirely different services by the White House. True or false?

51. Why did the White House use Hunt and Liddy for undercover work when it could have gone to the FBI?

52. Which of the following was *not* a term by which Hunt and Liddy referred to the Plumbers?
    a) Roto-Rooters
    b) Room 16
    c) Odessa

53. Each individual Plumber owed his position to connections with a White House superior, and hence represented that superior's interests and attitude. Match the Plumber to the appropriate White House official.
    a) Kissinger   1) Liddy
    b) Ehrlichman   2) Hunt
    c) Mitchell   3) Young
    d) Colson   4) Krogh

54. For which of the following were the Plumbers responsible?
    a) Bugging the Democratic National Committee
    b) Bugging the Chilean embassy
    c) Breaking into Daniel Ellsberg's psychiatrist's office
    d) All of the above

55. Finish Ehrlichman's lament about Kissinger and their respective roles with the Plumbers: "Kissinger gets the Nobel Prize and . . ."

56. Where did Hunt expect to get LSD?
    a) CIA
    b) Haight-Ashbury
    c) Colson

57. In a taped conversation in July 1971, Colson told Hunt that Ellsberg was getting support from "the real enemy" (meaning the Soviet Union). What does the tape reveal that Hunt assumed Colson meant by the "real enemy"?
    a) The Democratic National Committee
    b) Cuba
    c) SDS (Students for a Democratic Society)

58. How did Colson and Liddy plan to disrupt a Daniel Ellsberg fund-raiser in September 1971?
    a) Sneak in the Cubans dressed as waiters and drug Ellsberg's soup.
    b) Put out mimeographed invitations in local black neighborhoods promising free beer.
    c) Release dozens of vampire bats from the basement.

59. A memorandum from Ehrlichman to Colson dated August 27, 1971, requested a "game plan" on "Hunt-Liddy Special Project Number One." What was the project?

60. Which of the following was *not* a reason that Nixon believed accounted for FBI Director Hoover's apparent reluctance to press the investigation of Ellsberg?
    a) Hoover never passed up an opportunity to let Nixon know that Hoover ultimately held the high cards.
    b) Ellsberg's father was Hoover's friend.
    c) Ellsberg's father gave toys to FBI agents' children at Christmas.

61. Nixon ordered the break-in at the office of Daniel Ellsberg's psychiatrist. True or false?

62. Why would the CIA have given Hunt disguises and other assistance if he was not working for the CIA?
    a) Ehrlichman so requested.
    b) Hunt was still secretly working for the CIA.
    c) Hunt had friends at the CIA.

63. When Ehrlichman asked General Robert Cushman (Deputy Director of the CIA) to "lend a hand" to Hunt, why did Cushman

not ask if Hunt's mission involved an American citizen or would occur in the United States?

64. While waiting on a park bench at the scene of the Ellsberg break-in, Liddy abandoned his hippie wig disguise. Why?
   a) The wig became itchy.
   b) He couldn't see through the wig's bangs.
   c) He felt he was being cruised by a seven-foot-tall Navajo Indian homosexual.

65. How did the CIA get pictures of a grinning Liddy in front of the building where Ellsberg's psychiatrist had an office?
   a) The CIA followed the Plumbers.
   b) Hunt took the pictures with a camera lent by the CIA, and forgot about them when he returned the camera.
   c) The CIA knew that Ellsberg's psychiatrist had installed a surveillance system.

66. What was unusual about a pair of thick glasses and a piece of lead given to Liddy by the CIA for the Ellsberg job?

67. Liddy carried a knife during the Ellsberg break-in; he would not have used it to hurt anyone, however. True or false?

68. Who said the following to Assistant Attorney General Henry Petersen, then investigating the Watergate burglary, concerning the Ellsberg break-in: "I know about that. That is a national security matter. . . . Your mandate is to investigate Watergate"?
   a) Nixon
   b) L. Patrick Gray
   c) Kissinger

69. Dean reported that the President was angered at the supposed contents of Morton Halperin's safe (Halperin was a former staff member of the National Security Council, who was then working for the Brookings Institution). Who ordered "everyone to rifle" his files and "get 'em back"?
   a) Nixon
   b) Colson
   c) Liddy

70. Besides antiwar activities, what other reason did the White House have for continuing its wiretapping of Morton Halperin long after he had left the White House?
    a) There was evidence that Halperin was contacting North Vietnamese agents.
    b) Halperin became a member of Democratic presidential candidate Muskie's foreign-policy staff.
    c) Wiretap summaries revealed that Halperin was going to release false information concerning the U.S. role in Vietnam.

71. How did Colson plan to get his hands on Morton Halperin's documents, which were then kept in the Brookings Institution?

72. How did Hunt and Liddy intend to break into the Brookings Institution?

73. According to Liddy, why didn't the White House approve the plan?
    a) Haldeman was afraid that the Cubans would not be convincing firemen.
    b) The White House was too cheap to buy a fire engine.
    c) The Brookings Institution's extensive sprinkler system would put out any fire almost immediately.

74. Nixon was aware of Colson's proposed plan to firebomb the Brookings Institution. True or false?

Deep Throat Question
75. What member of the Nixon Administration said, ". . . you'll find that Liddy and Hunt had reputations that are the lowest. The absolute lowest. Hiring these two was immoral. They got exactly what they wanted."

☆2☆

CREEP

"We were faced . . . by an organization that had . . . unlimited money, that was led by the most ruthless group of political operatives ever mobilized for a presidential campaign." —*Richard Nixon, writing about the 1960 presidential campaign*

"Nobody gets anything back as far as the general contributions are concerned in this Administration. Second, as far as those who receive them are concerned, they must be accepted with no misunderstandings expressed or implied, that anything is to be done, as a result of those contributions, that would not be done in the ordinary course of events."
—*President Nixon, March 27, 1973*

"I say it was morally wrong if the money was secretly given and secretly handled. And I say it was morally wrong if any of the contributors got special favors for the contributions that they made."
—*President Nixon, September 23, 1952, The "Checkers speech"*

"I don't know what's going on in this campaign and I don't think you ought to try to know." —*Maurice Stans (CREEP finance chairman) to Hugh Sloan, April 7, 1972*

15

THE TIMES *(1968–1972)*

The presidential races in 1960 and 1968 had been extremely close. Nixon always believed that the 1960 race was stolen away by a group that not only out-campaigned him but was better at "dirty tricks."

Soon after the 1968 election, Nixon and his inner core decided that the next election would be no nail-biter. The field of solid Democratic contenders promised a tough fight, however. Rather than trust the Republican party to run his campaign, Nixon set the party machinery adrift and formed his own personal committees, the Committee to Re-Elect the President (CREEP) and the Finance Committee to Re-Elect the President. Most CREEP staffers simply moved over from their White House offices. The committees' goal was to guarantee Nixon's reelection.

The Finance Committee apparently believed it impossible to raise adequate funds legally, and therefore relied on secret fund-raising, slush funds, contribution laundering in Mexico, dummy committees, and strongarm tactics. Large corporations were favorite targets. The carrot of favorable (and stick of unfavorable) future treatment by the Administration compelled many executives to turn over corporate funds illegally to "avoid being on the bottom of the totem pole," in the words of Gulf Oil lobbyist Claude Wilde. The fund-raising was spectacularly successful.

Outright sabotage succeeded mere political spying in the last year before the election; the targets now were Democrats, not just left-wingers. The early success of the infamous "Canuck letter" in the New Hampshire primary, which falsely accused Democratic candidate Edmund Muskie of racial slurs, seemed to finish Muskie's candidacy almost instantly. CREEP operatives led by Donald Segretti hired numerous students to accelerate the intelligence and sabotage directed against Democratic candidates. Finally, the Plumbers were dragooned into the election-year fray to carry out an ambitious scheme of high-level sabotage.

QUESTIONS

1. According to Major General Edward Lansdale, what did Nixon say in 1968 to him after he (Lansdale) told him he was in charge of

making the election in Vietnam "the most honest election that has ever been held in Vietnam"?
a) "That's great, but don't overlook our candidate, if you know what I mean."
b) "Oh, sure, honest, yes, honest, that's right—so long as you win."
c) "Why don't you talk to Murray Chotiner? He's helped me in all my campaigns."

2. During the 1962 Nixon-Brown gubernatorial campaign, which Nixon Administration officials created a phony voters' poll and a dummy organization called the "Committee for the Preservation of the Democratic Party in California" that contacted Democrats to say that Brown was an extremist?

3. Who stated in an August 1972 memorandum to White House staffers that he had indeed once said, "I would walk over my grandmother if necessary" to assure the President's reelection?
a) Colson
b) Hunt
c) Magruder

4. During the Watergate investigation, young staffers at syndicated columnist Jack Anderson's office got on several telephones and made a gag call to Chuck Colson's office. Who did they announce was calling?
a) Judge Sirica
b) Colson's grandmother
c) Assistant Fire Chief Brookings

5. Guess Colson's response to the caller.
a) "I don't have a grandmother."
b) "Listen, wise guy, you ought to know better than to pull a dirty trick on me."
c) "I'm sure the Lord in His merciful wisdom will forgive you this tasteless joke."

6. What did Liddy say upon hearing of Colson's religious conversion?
a) "Does he think Sirica will fall for this born-again bull?"

b) "If he'd run over his grandmother for Nixon, imagine what he'll do for Jesus."

c) "That man is just not screwed on right. He's a little nuts."

7. Finance chairman Stans took a high-powered, high-pressure fund-raising trip through the Southwest just before the new April 7 contribution-disclosure law became effective. What was the trip humorously called by some?

   a) "Stans's Shakedown Cruise"
   b) "Maury's Money Run"
   c) "The Trick or Treat Trip"

8. Prankster Dick Tuck planned a dirty trick to highlight Nixon's fund-raising methods by hiring a Brink's truck to drive away from John Connally's ranch after a fund-raiser. What sort of vehicle was to follow the Brink's truck?

   a) A prison van
   b) A Mexican laundry truck
   c) A hearse

9. What was CREEP's procedure for getting around the gift-tax law that allowed no more than a $3,000 contribution gift-tax-free?

10. What did the Volunteers for Effective Government, Active Friends of a Balanced Society, United Friends of Good Government, and Supporters of the American Dream have in common?

11. What was CREEP's procedure to get around the prohibition against corporate contributions?

12. Although CREEP shook money out of corporations, it wasn't able to get advertising agencies or public-relations firms to funnel corporate contributions to CREEP. True or false?

13. The selling of ambassadorships also proved a valuable fund-raising device. Luxembourg proved more expensive than Finland. True or false?

14. How did CREEP launder funds?

15. Stans denied that funds were being laundered. True or false?

16. What was the nickname for laundered funds?
    a) "Chiquita bananas"
    b) "Tex-Mex checks"
    c) "Wetback greenbacks"

17. Which one of the following men was *not* in charge of a CREEP slush fund?
    a) Sloan
    b) Stans
    c) Haldeman
    d) Kalmbach

18. Which one of the following men was *not* a contributor to Bebe Rebozo's private "little tin box"?
    a) Howard Hughes
    b) Dwayne Andreas
    c) J. Paul Getty
    d) Stewart Mott

19. When the famous $25,000 Dahlberg check (part of the funds to finance the Watergate burglary) was traced to CREEP's counsel, Liddy, by Woodward and Bernstein, what was CREEP's explanation?
    a) It was an honest mistake.
    b) The contribution was made before the new law was effective.
    c) Liddy was investigating measures to counter an attack by crazies on Nixon at the convention.

20. The Associated Milk Producers, Inc., promised Nixon a contribution for the 1972 campaign in return for action to curb dairy imports, but such action was never taken. True or false?

21. Nixon stated the following to representatives of milk industry groups: "And I must say a lot of businessmen and others I get around this table, they yammer and talk a lot but they don't do anything about it. But you and I appreciate that. I don't need to spell it out." True or false?

22. Nixon said publicly that the subject of campaign contributions had not been raised with the Associated Milk Producers. True or false?

23. What happened to the price of milk right after the dairy cooperative contributed $422,500 to CREEP?

24. How did the $250,000 contribution to CREEP from Amerada Hess Oil benefit the corporation?

25. On December 7, 1971, W. Clement Stone, chairman of the board of Combined Insurance Company of Chicago, dined at the White House. On December 8, 1971, his company asked for an exemption from the price board on insurance premiums (a wage-price freeze was then in effect), which he received within two weeks. How much did Stone contribute to CREEP?

26. Early in August, both major political parties released figures for the amounts of money expected to be raised between April 7 and election day. Match the expected figure to the party.
    a) $2–3 million   1) Republican
    b) $20 million   2) Democratic
    c) $35 million
    d) $40 million

27. How much did the Finance Committee to Re-Elect the President ultimately collect?

28. How soon after Nixon's election in 1969 did Haldeman put the first Nixon spy on the secret White House payroll?
    a) Two days
    b) Two months
    c) Nearly a year

29. In April 1971, Nixon reviewed a series of task force proposals for the 1972 campaign, everything from an advertising task force to a political strategy task force. What task force (missing from the plan presented to Nixon) did Nixon order Haldeman to implement right away?
    a) Task Force on Campaign Intelligence
    b) Task Force on Financing
    c) Task Force on Foreign Policy Formulation

30. CREEP's original scheme for campaign intelligence contained no plans for electronic surveillance. True or false?

31. CREEP's first campaign intelligence plan called for, among other things, outfitting a New York apartment as a boudoir in which to seduce the women at Teddy Kennedy's Chappaquiddick party. What was the name of the plan?
   a) Operation Sandwedge
   b) Operation Teddy Bare
   c) Operation Bedmake

32. White House undercover agent Tony Ulasewicz believed the hardest way to obtain information from the Democratic party was to write and ask for it. True or false?

33. Which of the following lines of inquiry was *not* undertaken by Caulfield at the request of Ehrlichman?
   a) Possible financial links between Sen. Edward Muskie and corporations with significant pollution problems
   b) A possible homosexual affair involving the brother of a presidential candidate
   c) The Chappaquiddick incident
   d) Possible questionable financial dealings by George Wallace

34. On January 7, 1972, Liddy presented Mitchell with a far-reaching $1 million plan that called for chase planes, prostitutes, commandoes, and microwave interception in order to obtain intelligence about the plans of the Democratic candidates. True or false: The CIA made the charts for Liddy's presentation.

35. What was the code name of Liddy's intelligence plan?

36. The first two meetings during which Liddy proposed his elaborate surveillance plans were not held in the White House. True or false?

37. At the first meeting wherein Liddy presented his intelligence plan, how did he verify to Mitchell that he could assure him of "the finest call girls in the country" as part of the intelligence-gathering scheme?
   a) CIA sources
   b) Résumés of operatives
   c) First-hand experience

38. Part of Liddy's intelligence scheme involved a counter-demonstration plan based on kidnapping radical leaders. Which of the following did Liddy *not* plan to do with the kidnapped leaders?
    a) Drug them
    b) Threaten their families
    c) Detain them in Mexico

39. What did John Mitchell say to Liddy about his plan for "mugging squads," kidnapping, etc.?
    a) "Outrageous"
    b) "Criminal"
    c) "Not realistic"

40. Why did Magruder and Mitchell feel compelled to press on with Liddy's intelligence scheme?
    a) Haldeman insisted on better information concerning the alleged Howard Hughes–Larry O'Brien connection.
    b) They were afraid that if they didn't press on, Colson would take over the plan and screw it up.
    c) Time was running out before the election, and Nixon was eager for inside intelligence.

41. What did Mitchell say when Sam Dash, counsel to the Senate Watergate Committee, asked why Mitchell didn't throw Liddy out of his office when he presented the intelligence scheme.

42. Why did Mitchell and Liddy consider breaking into Las Vegas publisher Hank Greenspun's office?

43. With respect to the proposed break-in of Hank Greenspun's office, what arrangements did Liddy tell McCord had been made for the burglars' escape?

44. The White House's "dirty tricks" began in connection with the 1972 campaign. True or false?

45. The overall purpose of the dirty tricks perpetrated against the 1972 Democratic presidential candidates was to see to it that George McGovern would be the Democratic presidential nominee. True or false?

46. Ehrlichman publicly deemed appropriate the use of private investigators to probe the sexual and drinking habits, domestic problems, and social activities of political candidates for use in campaigns. True or false?

47. George Bush, the Republican National Chairman, publicly supported Ehrlichman's opinion as set forth in the previous question. True or false?

48. What famous appointment book did Caulfield obtain, but then not use, because too many Republican politicians were also listed in it?

49. The revelation in the press about Democratic vice-presidential candidate Eagleton's history of mental problems surprised Nixon insiders as much as it surprised Democratic insiders. True or false?

50. How did Colson suggest to Hunt that CREEP might be able to use Bremer's attempted assassination of George Wallace to Nixon's advantage?

51. During the campaign, McGovern tried hard, but failed, to win the endorsement of the AFL-CIO. The head of the labor organization, George Meany, was upset at receiving a telephone call from someone who identified himself as Gary Hart (McGovern's campaign manager) and demanded that Meany present himself at a specified time and place to meet McGovern. True or false: Meany suspected the call was a "dirty trick."

52. Haldeman received a memorandum from CREEP staffer Ronald Walker stating that about two hundred violent and obscene demonstrators would show up for Nixon's visit to Charlotte the next day. Haldeman wrote "Good" in the margin. Further on, however, Walker stated that the demonstration would not only be directed against the President, but against evangelist Billy Graham as well. What was Haldeman's marginal notation?
    a) "Not against Graham!"
    b) "See if you can stop this."
    c) "Great."

53. What high-ranking Nixon Administration official suggested to Sen. James Buckley that he stage a demonstration against himself in which he would be physically threatened?

54. Haldeman wrote a memo to Dean dated February 10, 1973, which stated, "We need to get our people to put out the story on the foreign or communist money that was used in support of demonstrations against the President in 1972. We should tie all 1972 demonstrations to McGovern and thus to the Democrats as part of the peace movement which leads directly to McGovern and Teddy Kennedy." When this memorandum was produced at the Ervin committee hearings, what evidence did Haldeman offer the committee to support the statements in the memo?

55. What was the purpose of falsifying State Department cables to pin the assassination of Diem on John F. Kennedy?
   a) To blame the Vietnam War on the Democrats
   b) To tarnish the memory of President Kennedy
   c) To get Kissinger to participate in "dirty tricks"

56. Who said the following on September 16, 1971: "I would remind all concerned that the way we got into Vietnam in the first place was through overthrowing Diem and the complicity in the murder of Diem"?
   a) Nixon
   b) Hunt
   c) Kissinger

57. Why was Hunt's taped interview with a certain Lieutenant Colonel Conein unsuccessful in supporting Hunt's claim that President Kennedy ordered Diem's assassination?
   a) Conein had never been to Vietnam.
   b) Conein refused to cooperate after learning of Hunt's scheme.
   c) Conein got drunk and sat on Hunt's tape recorder, crushing it.

58. Why would Colson's plan to have *Life* magazine print an exposé of John F. Kennedy's supposed order to assassinate Diem have failed?
   a) Colson knew *Life* would recognize the cables as fakes.
   b) *Life* would protect the Kennedys regardless.
   c) *Life* was about to cease publication.

59. As part of his "get Teddy" campaign, what sort of photo of Teddy Kennedy did Nixon most want Colson to come up with?

60. A retired army general told Bob Woodward of *The Washington Post* that he saw some TV commercials showing a buxom blonde sitting on Ted Kennedy's lap, which CREEP planned to use against him in the last days of a campaign should he run against Nixon. Where would CREEP get such a picture?
    a) From Hunt's old cronies at the CIA
    b) From J. Edgar Hoover's private files
    c) By faking it

61. Referring to CREEP dirty tricks, who said the following to Bob Haldeman: "Maybe I started it, but you guys ran it into the ground"?

62. The Trojan Knights Political Club flourished at the University of Southern California. Among its activities were stealing opposition candidates' leaflets, ripping down opposition candidates' posters, and stuffing ballot boxes. Which one of the following men was *not* a former member of the Trojan Knights?
    a) Chapin
    b) Segretti
    c) Strachan
    d) Ziegler

63. What was Donald Segretti's term to describe political sabotage?
    a) "Ratfucking"
    b) "Mindfucking"
    c) "Black operation"

64. Which of the following were *not* Segretti dirty tricks?
    a) Stealing important documents from campaign headquarters
    b) Forging campaign literature
    c) Contriving phony press releases
    d) Sending numerous extra tickets to fund-raisers
    e) Kidnapping campaign workers
    f) Posing as gay activists and starting fights at Democratic rallies
    g) Shadowing and compiling dossiers on candidates' families
    h) Taking out nominating petitions for phony candidates

i) Infiltrating candidates' headquarters

j) Putting stink bombs in candidates' headquarters

k) Paying demonstrators to show up at rallies with political competitors' posters

65. What phony award did Segretti suggest publicly awarding to Teddy Kennedy?

66. Which of the following was *not* one of the false charges Segretti included in the so-called sex letters during the Florida primary?

a) Scoop Jackson had fathered an illegitimate child.

b) Scoop Jackson had been arrested on homosexual charges.

c) Humphrey had fathered an illegitimate child.

d) Humphrey had been arrested for drunk driving.

67. What was the reaction of Dwight Chapin, Nixon's appointment secretary, when Segretti told him of the phony "sex letters" composed on Muskie stationery and mailed three days before the Florida primary in March 1972?

68. One of Segretti's agents hired a woman to parade naked in front of a hotel where Muskie was staying and scream, "Muskie, I love you!" True or false?

69. Fill in the blank in the quotation below, taken from a poster created, prepared, and mailed by Segretti.
"Help Muskie Support Busing Our Children Now."
Sponsored by _____

a) Busers for Muskie

b) Mothers for Busing

c) Children's Crusade for Busing

70. Fill in the blank in the quotation below, printed on a streamer towed behind an airplane hired by Segretti and flown over the 1972 Democratic convention.
"Peace, _____, Promiscuity; Vote McGovern."

a) Parole

b) Permissiveness

c) Pot

71. What message was on the ribbons tied to the mice that Segretti let loose at a Muskie press conference?
    a) "Muskie Is a Rat Fink."
    b) "Don't Rat Out on America; Vote McGovern."
    c) "We Left a Sinking Ship; Vote Jackson."

72. For a Muskie fund-raiser in Washington, Segretti ordered large quantities of pizza, flowers, liquor, and even a magician, in the name of the organizer. What live animal did Segretti try to send?
    a) Monkey
    b) Donkey
    c) Elephant

73. Fill in the blank in the quotation below, which was printed by Segretti on cards distributed at a Wallace rally just before the Florida primary.
    "If you like _____, you'll love Wallace
    . . . Vote for Muskie."
    a) Bishop Sheen
    b) John Birch
    c) Hitler

74. Segretti, Hunt, and Liddy so loved their quasi-espionage life-style that they could not resist code-naming (even double-code-naming) their operatives. Match the operative with his code name.
    a) Sedan Chair   1) John Buckley
    b) Fat Jack   2) Thomas Gregory
    c) Ruby I   3) Michael McMinoway
    d) Ruby II

75. Which one of the following was *not* an alias used by Segretti?
    a) Bill Mooney
    b) Mitch Midita
    c) Dan Simmons

76. What important piece of campaign intelligence did "Sedan Chair" overhear Frank Mankiewicz discussing?
    a) Bart Porter's perjury before the grand jury

b) Senator Eagleton's health before he was chosen as vice-presidential nominee

c) Mankiewicz's ability to finger Segretti as the perpetrator of CREEP dirty tricks

77. Thirty-one-year-old Ken Reitz spent the 1972 campaign as CREEP's national college director, but really he was serving as a central repository for the intelligence unearthed by Segretti's and Gorton's college-kid spies. What important post in the Republican party had Haldeman already slotted for Reitz?

78. Who were "Pissers for McGovern"?

79. Why didn't Mitchell like the "Pissers" plan?

Deep Throat Questions

80. Why did CREEP take pains never to mention Nixon's name during the 1972 campaign?

81. Match the "intelligence" activity with Liddy's code word in his original $1 million "Gemstone" intelligence plan.

a) Counter-demonstration plan	1) Diamond
b) Infiltration by spies	2) Emerald
c) A plan to funnel money to Shirley Chisholm to make the Democrats fight over a black woman candidate	3) Coal
d) A chase plane to eavesdrop on Democratic candidates' aircraft	4) Ruby
e) Microwave interception of telephone traffic	5) Sapphire
f) Electronic surveillance	6) Crystal
g) Prostitutes to compromise politicians	7) Quartz
h) "Black-bag" operations to plant bugs	8) Opals I–IV
i) Photographs of documents	9) Turquoise
j) Counter-demonstrations in favor of Democrats by repulsive people	10) Garnet
k) A commando team of Cubans to destroy air conditioning at the Democratic Convention	11) Topaz

1.

2.

3.

4.

5.

6.

Photo I.D. Quiz #1

82. What was the "town house operation"?

83. Trace the $25,000 contribution initially made by Dwayne Andreas to Ken Dahlberg, which ended up in the bank account of Watergate burglar Bernard Barker.

84. Did Andreas receive anything in return for his contribution?

85. Who was Paul Morrisson of Deerfield Beach, Florida?

☆3☆

THE BREAK-IN

"By God, [Nixon's] got some former CIA men working for him that I'd kick out of my office. Some day that bunch will serve him up a fine mess."
—*J. Edgar Hoover, Spring 1972,*
just before his death in May

"My boys got caught last night. I made a mistake. . . . I am afraid I'm going to lose my job."
—*G. Gordon Liddy to Hugh Sloan, June 18, 1972*

THE TIMES *(June 17, 1972)*

The crew that invaded the Democratic National Headquarters to plant electronic devices for political espionage was commanded by two White House Plumbers, the crypto-Nazi Liddy and the romantic-thriller author Hunt. Needing support to pull off the burglary, Hunt had combed the ranks of Cuban exiles, soldiers of fortune, anti-Castroists, and veterans of the Bay of Pigs fiasco. Joined by former CIA agent James McCord (then director of security for CREEP) and the Cubans, these curious and bizarre swashbunglers fumbled their way into the Watergate and the history books . . . and got caught. Probably it was their arrogance (after all, they were "experienced" secret agents) as much as careless planning and slipshod execution that did them in.

Precisely why the sought-after information was valuable enough to justify the risk has never been satisfactorily explained. In any case, Attorney General Mitchell, who had been disappointed with one nonfunctioning device and the quality of the information from the previously planted bugs, blasted Liddy about it. So McCord took the boys back in.

QUESTIONS

---

1. What presidential candidate did J. Edgar Hoover tell Nixon he (Hoover) had had the FBI bug during the 1968 campaign?

2. James McCord was once the "number-one man" in charge of security at the CIA. True or false?

3. What was McCord's first duty as the new chief of security for CREEP?
   a) To help Liddy plan burglaries
   b) To keep the Democrats from breaking in
   c) To keep Martha Mitchell secure

4. At the high point of his law-enforcement career, which Watergate felon arrested Dr. Timothy Leary in a drug bust?
   a) Hunt
   b) Liddy
   c) Sturgis

5. Which Watergate felon won a Guggenheim Fellowship?
   a) Hunt
   b) Liddy
   c) Barker

6. Liddy predicted that after the presidential election, he would become the leader of a soon-to-be-established clandestine White House police force. True or false?

7. Which of the following courtroom stunts did Liddy *not* perform when trying cases as an assistant district attorney in New York?
   a) He shattered the courtroom railing with a two-by-four.
   b) He shot a hole in the courtroom ceiling.
   c) He kicked a chair across the courtroom.

8. During his CIA spy days, Hunt was involved in which of the following?
   a) An aborted assassination attempt on Panamanian dictator Torrijos
   b) The overthrow of the Arbenz regime in Guatemala
   c) The Bay of Pigs

9. Liddy ran for Congress in 1968; which of the following describes his key campaign poster?
   a) A faked photograph of him confronting a crowd of unruly blacks
   b) A photograph of him dressed as Wyatt Earp, blowing smoke from a recently fired pistol
   c) A photograph of him dressed as a state trooper holding a bull-horn in front of a police cruiser

10. What celebrated response did Liddy give to Magruder after Magruder put his arm on Liddy's shoulder to offer friendly advice?
    a) "Please be so kind as to remove your arm from my shoulder and watch out for your own ass."
    b) "If you ever put your arm on me again, I'm going to break it off your shoulder and beat you to death with it."
    c) "My own father learned quickly not to touch me, ever. Remember that."

11. At the celebrated West Coast dinner in 1972 where Liddy demonstrated his will, what did Liddy ignite that so shocked his dinner companions?
    a) Magruder's necktie
    b) A firecracker
    c) His own hand

12. Which of the burglars gave his secretary a six-by-four-foot poster of himself standing beside a police car and holding a bullhorn?
    a) Hunt
    b) Liddy
    c) McCord

13. While casing McGovern headquarters in preparation for a break-in, how did Liddy solve the problem of the brightly lit alley next door?
    a) He suggested a daytime entry with operatives disguised as maintenance men.
    b) He told student Thomas Gregory to infiltrate the campaign and let them in at night.
    c) He shot out the lights.

14. While he was a Plumber, Liddy enjoyed screening old Nazi propaganda films in the White House basement. True or false?

15. Match the alias or nickname with the burglar.
    a) Edward Hamilton   1) Howard Hunt
    b) Frank Carter   2) Gordon Liddy
    c) Jean Valdes   3) James McCord
    d) Raul Godoyn   4) Bernard Barker
    e) Edward Martin   5) Virgilio Gonzalez
    f) George Leonard   6) Eugenio Martinez
    g) Ed Warren   7) Frank Sturgis
    h) Eduardo   8) Alfred Baldwin
    i) Macho
    j) Musculo
    k) Moe Johnson
    l) Frank Fiorini
    m) Bill Johnson
    n) Manolo

16. Which of the Cubans joined Castro and was even tapped by him to oversee Cuba's gambling operations, yet participated in the Bay of Pigs, founded the International Anti-Communist Brigade in the 1960s to invade Cuba, and dropped anti-Castro leaflets over Cuba from a B-25 maintained by Hunt?

17. Which of the Cubans fought in World War II with the Army Air Corps, was a POW in a Nazi prison camp for seventeen months, later joined Batista's secret police, yet left to sign on with Castro in the 1950s, served as CIA paymaster for the Bay of Pigs operation, and later worked with Hunt, dropping leaflets over Cuba from a B-25?

18. Which of the Cubans fought with Castro, fled to Miami, and was the only one identified as still on the CIA's payroll at the time of the Watergate burglary?

19. Which of the Cubans was a former member of Cuban dictator Batista's secret police and, because of his expertise with locks, was specially flown in for the Ellsberg break-in?

20. According to Jack Anderson, which one of the following men was *not* at one time or another reportedly involved in a real-estate deal with Bebe Rebozo?
    a) Nixon
    b) Mitchell
    c) Barker
    d) Martinez

21. In 1960, Bebe Rebozo opened a bank in Key Biscayne. For which of the following was the bank *not* known by the time Nixon was elected in 1968?
    a) Its first savings-account customer was Nixon.
    b) It was a haven for stolen stocks channeled by organized crime.
    c) It was a favorite of the right-wing Cuban exile community.
    d) It was the choice of cash-rich international drug financiers.

22. How soon after the assassination of John Kennedy was Frank Sturgis approached by an FBI agent who said to him, "If there's

anybody capable of killing the President of the United States, you're the guy who can do it"?
a) Immediately
b) Two weeks
c) Six months

23. In connection with the assassination of John Kennedy, which Watergate figures were once identified as the "mystery tramps" arrested near the "grassy knoll" at the site of the shooting?

24. The Cubans were paid $10,000 a piece for their participation in the burglary. True or false?

25. What Cuban participated in the Ellsberg break-in but not in the Watergate break-in?

26. Though Pico and De Diego were not recruited for the Watergate burglary, what conspiracy did they admit to the *Miami Herald* they had participated in?
a) Buying identical pairs of pajamas in a Washington shop
b) Breaking into embassies
c) Breaking into the office of Daniel Ellsberg's psychiatrist

27. What did Hunt testify that Liddy had told him was the reason for staging the break-in at DNC headquarters?
a) To find derogatory information on Democrats
b) To find derogatory information that the Democrats had on Republicans
c) To find information proving that Cuba was financing Democratic candidates

28. Attorney General Mitchell did not know about the break-in in advance. True or false?

29. Who did Ehrlichman once say was "more than a match for any lie-detector machine"?
a) Colson
b) Magruder
c) Strachan

30. Which Nixon White House aide took a lie-detector test to prove he had no prior knowledge of the Watergate break-in?
    a) Colson
    b) Magruder
    c) Strachan

31. What international financier told ABC-TV that at least six months before the Watergate scandal became public, he refused an offer to take part in a well-calculated plan to set up the impeachment of President Nixon?
    a) Robert Vesco
    b) Jacques Sarlie
    c) Howard Hughes

32. McCord and the burglars rented rooms for several days in the Howard Johnson's hotel across the street from the Watergate complex. How did McCord sign the register?
    a) McCord Associates, Inc.
    b) Mr. Edward L. Martin, Esq.
    c) Bill Singer

33. How many times did the Watergate burglars attempt to plant a bug in the Democratic National Committee headquarters before they were successful?
    a) Two
    b) Eleven
    c) Three

34. Michael Richardson, a photographic processor, developed two rolls of film given to him by Barker and Sturgis a week before the June 17 break-in. Aside from the fact that the photographs were of DNC documents, what was unusual about the prints?

35. "Gemstone" was the code name on the stationery on which the bugged conversations were transcribed. True or false?

36. The previously planted bug on Larry O'Brien's work phone turned out to have inadequate range and so couldn't be received in the Howard Johnson's hotel across the street. True or false?

37. Who was the DNC secretary who angered Mitchell by tying up the bugged phone in DNC headquarters with spicy romantic gossip?
    a) Maxie
    b) Menopause Mary
    c) Sally Harmony

38. What did one of the plainclothesmen who were called to the scene by Watergate security remark on seeing lookout Baldwin standing on a Howard Johnson's balcony across the street?
    a) "You'd think the guy would call the police instead of just staring."
    b) "If he's a lookout then we may have company, then we have a problem."
    c) "You don't think he'll call the police, do you?"

39. From his lookout post across the street, Baldwin saw the cops arrive at the Watergate. Why didn't he use his walkie-talkie to warn the burglars?

40. Why would lookout Baldwin have been unable to warn the burglars with his walkie-talkie anyway?

41. Who was Bob Bennett?

42. What presumably informed individual told the Ervin committee that break-ins and bugging operations "are very difficult activities, those who do it have to be trained up to the minute," and that the Watergate break-in was "amateurish in the extreme"?
    a) Former FBI Director J. Edgar Hoover
    b) Former CIA Director Richard Helms
    c) Former Attorney General John Mitchell

43. What member of the Nixon Administration broke into the dean's office at his university to check his file on financial aid?

44. The President did not know of the break-in in advance. True or false?

Deep Throat Questions

45. Which of the burglars served another prison sentence after his Watergate sentence, and for what crime?

46. Which of the burglars' aliases came from Hunt's spy novels?

47. How did the burglars first attempt to get into DNC headquarters?

48. Who was Manuel Artimé?

49. Who said the following to Hunt, and when: "Does this mean I won't be going to Miami"?

☆4☆

THE COVER-UP

"This kind of activity has no place whatever in our electoral process or in our governmental process. And, as Mr. Ziegler has stated, the White House has had no involvement whatever in this particular incident."
— *President Nixon, June 22, 1972*

"What we need in Washington is a President who, instead of covering up, cleans up."
— *Richard Nixon, 1952 presidential campaign*

"We are in it together. This is a war. We take a few shots and it will be over. We will give them a few shots and it will be over. Don't worry. I wouldn't want to be on the other side right now. Would you? . . .

"You really can't sit and worry about it all the time. The worst may happen, but it may not. So you just try to button it up as well as you can and hope for the best, and remember basically the damn business is unfortunately to cut our losses." — *President Nixon to John Dean, September 15, 1972*

"My God, you are an ant. You are nothing. Do you realize that the whole course of history is going to be changed?" — *James Sharp, counsel to CREEP, to CREEP aide Bart Porter on the subject of Porter's perjury*

THE TIMES *(Summer–Winter 1972)*

The discovery of the break-in threatened to expose the entire web of political spying and sabotage just as the reelection effort was gearing up for the stretch run. It could have been fatal. No one involved considered anything but containment; coming clean was unthinkable.

From the moment of the arrest, CREEP staff and White House officials scurried about, shoring up the damage. Scenarios were proposed, scapegoats fingered. Records and documents were destroyed wholesale. White House and CREEP aides perjured themselves. The wagons were drawn up in a circle around the President.

Acting for the President, White House counsel John Dean attempted to divert or derail the numerous government investigations that poked at the fabric of the Nixon Administration. Dean attempted to manipulate the apparently credulous Henry Petersen at the Justice Department and the ambitious Pat Gray at the FBI to gut their agencies' investigations and the investigation of the Watergate grand jury. White House political pressure squelched the investigation by the House Banking and Currency Committee.

Dean coordinated the working and reworking of the "explanation" as damning evidence dribbled out to the press and the investigators. The White House denied all knowledge or complicity.

By the end of the summer, the cover-up appeared secure. The grand jury indicted only the seven burglars. Nixon privately congratulated Dean on a job well done and, as the tapes reveal, announced his determination to wreak vengeance on his enemies, who would benefit by trumpeting Watergate about the town.

Nevertheless, there were unsettling rumblings. Aggressive investigators from *The Washington Post*, aided by a cautious mole in the Administration ("Deep Throat"), kept the burglary and ancillary revelations before the public. Disgruntled burglar McCord wrote to his former bosses at the CIA, warning them that the White House was maneuvering to pin the rap for Watergate on the agency. The burglars demanded hush money from the White House, and they got it. CREEP officials raided their political slush funds to tamp down the smoldering feeling among the burglars that they had been betrayed and would walk the plank alone.

Watergate did not prevent an election landslide. Nixon got more than 60 percent of the popular vo̶t̶ ̶nd ne̶ ̶ ̶ ̶ ̶ ̶ ̶ electoral vote.

But the election was the last celebration enjoyed by the Administration, and it was soon chilled by the Watergate beast that clamored for attention.

In early January 1973, Congress chartered the Select Committee on Campaign Activities to investigate questionable campaign tactics discovered in the previous election. It soon took on the name of its chairman, Sen. Sam Ervin of North Carolina.

The prosecution of the Watergate burglars resulted in guilty pleas and convictions, but left a suspicious judge. None of the burglars made statements. The judge, however, announced his dissatisfaction with the prosecution in open court, asserting his belief that the entire Watergate story had not been told.

By the end of the winter, Hunt's distraught demands for more money, coupled with threats from other Watergate burglars, signaled to Dean that the cover-up was in imminent danger of coming unstuck.

QUESTIONS

1. Which newspaper was the only one to report the break-in on page one?
   a) *The Washington Post*
   b) *The Pittsburgh Post-Gazette*
   c) *The Los Angeles Times*

2. Nixon was afraid that Colson had been one of the burglars. True or false?

3. On hearing of the break-in, Haldeman thought Colson had been apprehended in Democratic headquarters. True or false?

4. At first, Ehrlichman thought Colson had set up the burglary. True or false?

5. According to Magruder, what was the first thing Attorney General Mitchell did upon hearing of the break-in and arrest?
   a) He called his lawyer.
   b) He called the President and told him everything was okay.
   c) He called to get McCord out of jail before he could be traced to CREEP.

6. Liddy tried to justify using McCord (chief of CREEP security) in the burglary on the grounds that Magruder cut his burglary budget so badly. True or false?

7. In informing Dean of the burglary, Liddy took the blame and offered to allow himself to be shot on a local street corner. True or false?

8. McCord thought he would not have any legal problems when he was caught, because Mitchell had approved the operation. True or false?

9. Who was the first member of the Nixon Administration (before Nixon or Ziegler) to say the following publicly: "There is no place in our campaign or in the electoral process for this type of activity [burglary] and we will not permit or condone it"?

10. Who first suggested publicly that the Watergate break-in might very well have been engineered by the Democrats to use against the Republicans?
    a) Nixon
    b) Agnew
    c) Ziegler

11. After the arrest of the burglars, Liddy concocted schemes (never undertaken) to fake other break-ins and blame them on the Democrats. True or false?

12. Did anyone at the White House seriously contemplate having the burglars flee the country?

13. Members of the Nixon Administration both publicly and privately had their own pet names for the break-in. Match the word or phrase with its user.
    a) "Prank"   1) Mardian
    b) "Caper"   2) Ehrlichman
    c) "Slight PR problem"   3) Nixon
    d) "Third-rate burglary attempt" 4) Ziegler
    e) "Little jamboree"   5) Haldeman

14. Immediately after the June 17 break-in, what did Liddy do with the remaining $100 bills used to finance the operation?
    a) He bought a ticket to Rio de Janeiro.
    b) He returned them to Bebe Rebozo.
    c) He shredded them.

15. What did Mitchell tell Magruder to do with the Gemstone documents?
    a) "Don't ever let them see the light of day."
    b) "Show them to the President."
    c) "Have a good fire."

16. Which one of the following did John Dean *not* find in Howard Hunt's safe on June 20 (three days after the break-in)?
    a) Electronic equipment
    b) Memoranda to Colson concerning the Plumbers
    c) A psychiatric study of Ellsberg
    d) Materials concerning the Pentagon Papers
    e) Classified State Department cables
    f) A list of major contributors to CREEP
    g) Forged cables implicating John Kennedy in the assassination of South Vietnamese President Diem

17. Which of the items in the preceding question were withheld by Dean and Fred Fielding from files in Hunt's safe turned over to the FBI?

18. What did Ehrlichman tell Dean to do with the documents in Dean's safe?

19. What did Ehrlichman suggest that Dean do with Hunt's electronic equipment?
    a) Get it back to the CIA
    b) Find out if any of the stuff was illegal
    c) "Deep six" it

20. Did Dean shred or "deep six" the documents?

21. What did Dean give Gray that was "political dynamite"?
    a) Forged State Department cables

b) A list of fees for ambassadorships
c) Colson's enemy list

22. What did Gray do with the "political dynamite"?
    a) He hid it in J. Edgar Hoover's special wall safe with access only to the Director.
    b) He burned it.
    c) He turned it over to the Ervin committee.

23. What did Hugh Sloan offer as a reason for destroying CREEP's fund-raising records?
    a) "We were obvious targets for political espionage."
    b) "Ehrlichman told me to."
    c) "Maury (Stans) has a photographic memory anyway."

24. Why was the inside of McCord's house blackened right after the break-in?

25. Mitchell justified attempting to keep the lid on Watergate, the Ellsberg break-in, and other dirty tricks and White House crimes because Nixon was a better candidate than any of the Democrats. True or false?

26. What was Mitchell's term to describe the break-in at Ellsberg's psychiatrist's office and other dirty tricks and crimes of White House aides?

27. What did Mitchell state at the Ervin hearings "would have been simpler" than arranging the cover-up for Watergate participants?
    a) "Had them plead guilty."
    b) "Sent them out of the country."
    c) "Shot them all."

28. Did the cover-up succeed?

29. Hunt believed throughout the cover-up that he and Liddy could flee and hide out with some banana-republic dictator, such as Somoza in Nicaragua. True or false?

30. What was Ehrlichman's reply when told that Mitchell intended to see him purged from the Administration after the 1972 election?

a) "He'll go before I do."

b) "Mitchell should have stayed with municipal bonds—they don't fight back."

c) "No chance, pipe-face."

31. Who was the first CREEP official to leave?

32. Mitchell retired as campaign director to spend more time with his wife and get away from the campaign. True or false?

33. White House Press Secretary Ziegler was not part of the cover-up. True or false?

34. In a phone call on June 22, Martha Mitchell told Helen Thomas of UPI that she had given her husband an ultimatum to get out of politics. What did Ms. Thomas say to Martha?

a) "Why don't we collaborate on a book?"

b) She said nothing—an RNC security guard ripped Martha's phone out of the wall.

c) "Then that means your husband was involved in Watergate."

35. How did Martha Mitchell characterize her status in a subsequent phone call to Helen Thomas of UPI when she said she was going to leave Mitchell because of "all the dirty things that go on in the campaign"?

a) ". . . shackled and manacled."

b) ". . . a political prisoner."

c) ". . . on my way to becoming a Democrat."

36. U.S. Attorney Earl Silbert (in charge of prosecuting Watergate crimes) made it difficult for Dean to keep up with the details of the Watergate investigation. True or false?

37. Dean believed that Assistant Attorney General Petersen was willing to keep him informed on the grand jury investigation because Petersen believed in Nixon. True or false?

38. As it is normal for witnesses to testify in person before a grand jury, Assistant Attorney General Petersen refused to allow Stans, Colson, Krogh, Young, and Colson's secretary to submit written statements instead of testifying in person. True or false?

39. How did Liddy respond to questions put to him by the grand jury in June?

40. With respect to Petersen's investigation of Watergate, Petersen honestly felt the investigation had been adequate. True or false?

41. In September, Petersen wrote to each member of the House Banking and Currency Committee, urging all of them to subpoena witnesses in the committee's investigation and to coordinate their investigation with his. True or false?

42. Did Dean have difficulty tracking the FBI's investigation of Watergate?

43. Why was Pat Gray given the nickname "Two-Day Gray" when he was acting director of the FBI?
    a) He spent so much time away from FBI headquarters campaigning for Nixon.
    b) He had little law-enforcement experience.
    c) He was slow to answer questions about the Watergate investigation.

44. To whom was Howard Baker referring when he said the following: "[They] have so much on each other, neither of them can breathe"?
    a) Nixon and former CIA Director Helms
    b) Nixon and Larry O'Brien
    c) Nixon and John Mitchell

45. Whose idea was it to have the CIA call the FBI to say "stop the investigation"?
    a) Nixon's
    b) Dean's
    c) Gray's

46. Why did Nixon think the CIA would cooperate by getting the FBI to halt the Watergate investigation?
    a) He was the President and had asked them to.
    b) The investigation would reveal embarrassing facts about the Bay of Pigs fiasco.
    c) Martinez was on the CIA payroll.

47. Which of the following requests did Dean *not* make of Deputy
    CIA Director Walters?
    a) Put the brakes on Pat Gray
    b) Help get the burglars out of the country
    c) Provide hush money for the burglars

48. What did Ehrlichman say to indicate his disappointment when
    Walters said that to involve the CIA would only compound the
    problem by involving the President directly?
    a) That maybe he was right and Walters should blame the thing
       on Hunt and Liddy
    b) That on that particular day, General Walters seemed to have
       forgotten how he had gotten to where he was
    c) That it was probably just as well to keep the President out of it

49. As a result of Haldeman's request, Walters actually got Pat Gray
    to hold back the investigation by claiming prejudice to CIA inter-
    ests. True or false?

50. Walters even put in writing the CIA's request to slow the FBI in-
    vestigation. True or false?

51. It would have been simple for the CIA to claim a national security
    problem with respect to Mexico, as the CIA had numerous covert
    operations under way there. True or false?

52. The CIA even agreed to Dean's plan to claim that the Watergate
    burglary was their operation, on the condition that the White
    House put the request in writing. True or false?

53. President Nixon himself directed the manipulation of the CIA to
    obstruct the FBI's Watergate investigation. True or false?

54. Early in July 1972, Pat Gray told Nixon that his own assistants
    were mortally wounding the President by trying to confuse the
    issue as to whether or not there was CIA interest in the people
    the FBI wanted to interview. Gray said that Nixon then hesitated.
    What did Gray report that Nixon said to him?
    a) "Pat, you continue to conduct your thorough and aggressive
       investigation."

b) "Pat, there's all kind of evidence that this is a CIA operation."

c) "Pat, why don't you investigate the Democrats too?"

55. At the preliminary hearing before Judge Sirica, what did the Cubans state was their profession?
   a) Anticommunists
   b) Plumbers
   c) White House security guards

56. McCord's first attorney adopted the position that the burglary was lawful. True or false?

57. Why did McCord make a motion to the court to have the government disclose any wiretap communication of him?

58. What did a *Washington Post* reporter overhear McCord saying to Judge Sirica at his arraignment?
   a) That the guy he was working for was a creep
   b) That he was a former employee of the CIA
   c) That he did the burglary, but was innocent

59. Why did Hunt think he had a strong legal defense?
   a) He was working for the President on a national security matter.
   b) He was not caught in the Watergate, and the Cubans would not talk; even if they did, it would be their word against his.
   c) He believed that much of the government's case was based on documents illegally seized from his safe.

60. Why was the lookout, Baldwin, never indicted?

61. The Government Accounting Office reported that it could find no violations by CREEP in its fund-raising. True or false?

62. How many times had the GAO previously found violations of the Campaign Finance Law in presidential elections since the law's inception in 1925?
   a) About once per election (ten times)
   b) Only twice before (1960, 1964)
   c) Never

63. On the day that CREEP filed its countersuit against the Democrats, charging O'Brien with using the federal courts as "an instrument for creating political headlines," a bugging device was found in Democratic party headquarters. True or false?

64. On August 27, 1972, Nixon held a press conference wherein he admitted technical violations of campaign financing laws by Republicans and Democrats alike, but denied complicity by CREEP or the White House and cited six investigations already under way, including one by the White House. Finish the following Nixon quote: "What really hurts in matters of this sort is not the fact that they occur because overzealous people in campaigns do things that are wrong. What really hurts is . . ."

65. Who was most surprised by the President's announcement in August 1972 that John Dean had made a report to him on Watergate that exonerated White House personnel?

66. How did Dean's assistant, Fred Fielding, react to the President's publicizing of the Dean report on Watergate?
    a) "Well, John, it looks like you're going to have to change the findings in your report."
    b) "Well, John, if I were you, I wouldn't write that report."
    c) "Well, John, I guess you better get busy and write a report."

67. What was Cover-up Conspiracy Plan Number One, hatched by Dean soon after the break-in?

68. How did Dean try to keep Cover-up Conspiracy Plan Number One going by involving the CIA even after the CIA refused to go along?

69. What was Dean's second Cover-up Conspiracy Plan, hatched in the fall of 1972, after the first plan proved unworkable?

70. Even though Dean suspected that it would be hard to keep Magruder out of the investigation, he figured that Liddy's nutty background might make Cover-up Conspiracy Plan Number Two work. True or false?

71. What was Cover-up Conspiracy Plan Number Three, hatched in the spring of 1973, after there was too much public information to make the second plan believable?

72. What was Cover-up Conspiracy Plan Number Four, hatched soon after the target of the third plan refused to accept sole responsibility?

73. How did Bob Woodward of *The Washington Post* signal Deep Throat that he wanted to see him?
    a) By moving a flowerpot containing a red flag to the rear of his balcony
    b) By putting an ad in the personals section of *The Washington Post*
    c) By calling his office and leaving a phone message for "Mr. Deethroe"

74. How did Deep Throat signal Bob Woodward that he wanted to see him?
    a) By telephoning *The Washington Post* and leaving a message from "Mr. Deethroe"
    b) By circling a page of Woodward's daily *New York Times*
    c) By putting an ad in the personals section of *The Washington Post*

75. In early October, *The Washington Post* printed a report that Attorney General Mitchell had control over a secret campaign fund in Stans's office. What was Mitchell's indelicate•admonishment concerning the publisher of the paper, Katherine Graham?

76. Nixon justified paying hush money to the Watergate burglars on grounds of national security. True or false?

77. Ehrlichman privately justified paying hush money in secret because he reasoned that the Democrats would do the same thing. True or false?

78. Herb Kalmbach, Nixon's personal attorney, asked Ehrlichman about his raising money for the Watergate burglary defendants:

"I'm looking right into your eyes . . . and it is absolutely necessary, John, that you tell me that John Dean has the authority, that it is a proper assignment and that I'll go forward on it." Ehrlichman told him, lawyer to lawyer, that the payments were proper and legal. True or false?

79. How did Nixon refer to the funds to be raised for the legal bills of the Watergate burglars?
    a) "Silence sawbucks"
    b) "Plumbers' helpers"
    c) "Cuban Defense Fund"

80. When Haldeman requested a receipt for hush-money payments made from his personal $350,000 slush fund, Fred LaRue agreed. True or false?

81. In delivering the hush money, middleman Tony Ulasewicz used code names for those involved. Match codes to names.
    a) "Writer"   1) Burglars
    b) "Script"   2) Hunt
    c) "Players"   3) Money

82. In securing the hush money, Ulasewicz used more code names. Match them up.
    a) Novak   1) Ulasewicz
    b) Mr. Bradford 2) Kalmbach
    c) Miller   3) Kalmbach and LaRue

83. What was the difference between a "warm drop" and a "cold drop"?

84. Which one of the following places was *not* a "cold drop" location for hush money?
    a) Luggage lockers at Union Station
    b) A phone booth in the lobby of the building where Hunt's lawyer had offices
    c) Luggage lockers at Washington National Airport

85. What did Fred LaRue say to Strachan as he was putting on gloves before counting the $280,000 in hush money that Strachan had

just delivered?
a) "I never saw you."
b) "My hands are cold."
c) "You can never be sure about germs on dollar bills."

86. Which Watergate conspirator used his wife as a courier for hush-money payments to Watergate defendants?
a) Hunt
b) Liddy
c) Dean

87. How did Hunt explain all the cash found on his wife when she died in a plane crash in Chicago?
a) She had gone to Chicago on a shopping spree.
b) She was going to invest in a Chicago motel.
c) After their experience with the CIA, they didn't trust banks.

88. Where did Tony Ulasewicz put the $75,000 given to him by Kalmbach to pay off Hunt?
a) In a child's lunchbox in his kitchen
b) In a savings account under an assumed name
c) In a hotel laundry bag

89. What term did Ulasewicz use to describe the hush money he paid to the Watergate conspirators?

90. Ulasewicz testified that he was unable to transfer the money to Hunt through the lawyers on the case, and that something was "becoming a problem." What was it?

91. When Hunt began raising his demands for money from $75,000 to $200,000 and more to come, Ulasewicz told Kalmbach not to worry but to stick it out. True or false?

92. What was a "Kalmbach comeback call"?

93. How much money was paid to the burglars?
a) More than $1,000,000
b) More than $100,000
c) More than $400,000

7.

8.

9.

10.

11.

12.

13.

14.

15.

Photo I.D. Quiz #2

94. Who received the following anonymous message: "The President's ability to govern is at stake. Another Teapot Dome scandal is possible, and the government may fall. Everybody is on track but you. You are not following the game plan"?
    a) Caulfield
    b) McCord
    c) Liddy

95. Who, in December 1972, wrote to White House operative John Caulfield (who had taken over Kalmbach's duties as hush-money dispenser): "I am sorry to tell you this, but the White House is bent on having the CIA take the blame for the Watergate. If they continue to pursue this course, every tree in the forest will fall and it will be a scorched earth. Jack, even you will be hurt in the fallout"?
    a) McCord
    b) Hunt
    c) Liddy

96. When McCord grew tired of talking to John Caulfield through Ulasewicz, they agreed to a meeting on the George Washington Parkway. What was McCord suggesting by reciting his rule of thumb that when one man in an operation goes to jail, "all who are involved must go"?

97. When Dean related to Caulfield that an offer of executive clemency to McCord, Hunt, et al., had come from "the highest levels of the White House," did Dean mean the President?

98. How did Prosecutor Silbert get McCord to talk a little after Liddy and Hunt refused to?
    a) He promised clemency.
    b) He threatened to indict McCord's wife as an accessory.
    c) He told McCord that Hunt had already talked.

Deep Throat Questions
99. What was the first identifiable piece of evidence to be uncovered that linked the burglars to CREEP?

100. Name at least ten Watergate figures who—even if at the order of a superior—burned, shredded, destroyed, caused the disappearance of, or otherwise tampered with Watergate-related files or evidence.

101. In planning his anonymous hush-money drops, Tony Ulasewicz insisted on using pay phones. How did he keep track of all the loose change for so many phone calls?

102. Helms wrote and initialed a memorandum to Deputy CIA Director Walters eleven days after the break-in, in which it was falsely stated that the CIA would stick to its request (when in fact it backed off) to the FBI not to expand the investigation because it might harm CIA operations. What is the significance of the fact that Helms still had the original copy in his personal files?

☆5☆

THE COVER-UP UNRAVELS

The rope has to tighten slowly around everyone's neck.
. . . You get ten times the evidence you need against the
Hunts and Liddys. . . . They may not talk right away, but
the grip is on them. Then you move up and do the same
thing at the next level."
                    —*Deep Throat to Woodward, Fall 1972*

"I will bring John Ehrlichman down to his knees and
put him in jail. I have done enough seamy things for him
and Krogh that they'd never survive."
                    —*Howard Hunt, Spring 1973*

"Now we have to take a look at that course of action.
First it is going to require approximately a million dollars
to take care of the jackasses in jail. That could be ar-
ranged."   —*President Nixon to Dean, March 21, 1973*

"Magruder should take a slide."
                    —*President Nixon, July 30, 1972*

"When I was a kid I was taught that the captain went
down with the ship, not threw the crew overboard."
                    —*Jeb Magruder, 1981*

"I was determined that we should get to the bottom of
the matter, and that the truth should be fully brought
out—no matter who was involved."
                    —*President Nixon, April 30, 1973*

THE TIMES *(Spring 1973)*

By March 1973, the cover-up was falling apart. Hunt threatened to reveal Ehrlichman's role in the Ellsberg burglary, and the White House could not meet his escalating demands for cash. McCord visited the Ervin committee investigators. The hastily spun web of White House perjury and half-truths was unraveling.

At this same time, Pat Gray startled the public by admitting to the destruction of evidence given to him by Dean during Senate hearings to confirm him as the new Director of the FBI. Nixon withdrew Gray from consideration.

The Administration was further damaged by revelations from the Securities and Exchange Commission's probe of Robert Vesco (who made illegal contributions to CREEP), and the sensational events surrounding the ITT deal with the Administration (including Hunt's cloak-and-dagger efforts to stifle an ITT lobbyist).

As the Ervin committee was completing preparations to hear its first witnesses, Nixon announced publicly that he would refuse to allow his aides to testify. On March 21, Dean warned Nixon personally of a "cancer on the presidency." Two days later, Judge Sirica released a letter written to him by convicted burglar McCord, which laid out McCord's knowledge of White House participation in the burglary and cover-up.

Reeling from blows on so many fronts, Nixon called upon Haldeman and Ehrlichman to adapt the cover-up. While increasing numbers of Nixon aides visited the prosecutors, and others were interrogated by the grand jury, the cover-up strategy was shifted to calculate which aides should be sacrificed to quiet the voracious Watergate beast.

In April, Dean abandoned the cover-up and went to the prosecutors. Kleindienst and Petersen made a secret visit to the President to tell him of Dean's visit and to recommend strongly that Nixon dump Haldeman and Ehrlichman. Nixon did so in a public address on April 30 wherein he stressed that he had been overworked and had not understood the depth of the cover-up until he personally took over the investigation in March.

By May 1973, the entire inner cadre of the White House had gone: Colson and Mitchell much earlier; Haldeman, Ehrlichman, and Dean that April. Nixon was left to carry on alone.

Later that month the indictment against Daniel Ellsberg for passing classified documents was dismissed on grounds of government misconduct.

QUESTIONS

1. In a memo to his lawyer, Hunt set a deadline for the payment of "all past and current financial requirements" and receipt of "credible assurances . . . of continued resolve to honor all commitments" if the defendants were to remain silent. Which one of the following four areas was *not* one in which, according to Hunt, "the administration . . . remained deficient in living up to its commitments"?
   a) Financial support
   b) Coming clean with the public
   c) Legal fees
   d) Pardon
   e) Rehabilitation

2. Did the phrase "Off the reservation" mean the same thing as "not following the game plan"?

3. Five days before the trial of the Watergate burglars began, Caulfield met McCord and told him that if the Administration got its back to the wall, it would "have to take steps to defend itself." What was McCord's response?
   a) "I have had a good life and my will is made out."
   b) "I have some friends at the Company (CIA) who would not find you amusing."
   c) "You'll never find me on some damn street corner like Liddy."

4. On March 19, 1973, McCord wrote to Judge Sirica about certain events surrounding the burglars' trial. Which one of the following was *not* one of the important points in the letter?
   a) Pressure had been applied to the defendants to plead guilty and to keep quiet.
   b) Perjury had occurred.
   c) Others were involved in Watergate.
   d) The CIA was involved.

5. After the letter that McCord wrote to Sirica was made public on March 23, 1972, Liddy refused to talk to the grand jury. How did the prosecutors convince the press that Liddy had talked?
   a) They issued a statement saying he had talked.
   b) They immediately subpoenaed more White House aides.
   c) They kept Liddy out of sight for several hours, allowing the press to conclude that he had talked.

6. What led Dean to see the President on March 21 and tell him of the "cancer on the presidency"?
   a) Hunt had escalated his demands for money.
   b) Dean felt that the cover-up was crumbling and he wanted to make sure he didn't become the fall guy.
   c) His wife, Mo, suggested it.

7. What did Dean hope to accomplish by his March 21 "cancer on the presidency" meeting with Nixon?
   a) To end the cover-up and come clean
   b) To put the blame on Mitchell and save his own hide
   c) To threaten Haldeman and the President

8. To what was Nixon referring when he said the following to Dean at the March 21 meeting: "It seems to me we have to keep the cap on the bottle that much, or we don't have any options. . . . Either that or it all blows right now"?
   a) Meeting Hunt's financial demands
   b) Slowing the investigation of the Ellsberg burglary
   c) Keeping the press diverted from Watergate

9. When Dean told Nixon on March 21 that raising blackmail money was dangerous and that "we just don't know about these things [laundering money, etc.]," Nixon's reaction was that Dean had gone to law school and damned well ought to know. True or false?

10. The tapes of March 21, 1973, conversations reveal that it was Nixon who raised the possibility of clemency for Hunt. True or false?

11. When the President said "No, it's wrong, that's for sure," on the March 21 tape, to what was he referring?

    a) Clemency
    b) Blackmail payments (hush money)
    c) Using priests to hide hush-money payments

12. On the March 21 tape, who is revealed as saying, "When it breaks, it'll look like the President is covering up"?

13. Which one of the following was not an option set forth by Nixon on the March 21 tape to deal with Watergate?
    a) Grant Hunt parole instead of clemency
    b) Pardon Hunt, Liddy, and McCord, but not the Cubans
    c) Use priests to hide hush-money payments
    d) "Wash" money through New York or Las Vegas bookies
    e) Convene a grand jury and have Nixon men plead the Fifth
    f) Convene a grand jury and have Nixon men forget
    g) Co-opt the Assistant Attorney General by appointing him Special Prosecutor

14. How did Gray persuade Nixon to nominate him as FBI Director?
    a) Gray convinced Nixon that he was the most qualified man.
    b) Gray convinced Nixon that he owed him something for his help with the campaign.
    c) Gray convinced Nixon that he needed Gray at the FBI to keep the lid on things.

15. Who told Pat Gray to refuse to answer any more questions about Watergate during his FBI confirmation hearings?
    a) Nixon
    b) Higher-ups at the FBI
    c) Attorney General Kleindienst

16. During his confirmation hearings, Pat Gray said he received a "buck-up" call from Nixon concerning all the criticism he was taking and saying that there would always be a place for him in the Nixon Administration and "there'll be another . . ."
    a) ". . . way to string those guys up—our way."
    b) ". . . way to work with this Administration."
    c) ". . . day to get back at our enemies."

17. As Pat Gray began to lose his struggle for confirmation as Director of the FBI, what was Ehrlichman's famous "gallows re-

mark" about the degree of aid Gray could expect from the White House?

18. Soon after the Gray confirmation hearings and the voluntary withdrawal of his name from consideration, Gray told Petersen he had admitted to Senator Weicker that he had destroyed documents. Petersen responded, "Pat, I'm scared." What individuals did Petersen then say were apparently "expendable"?
   a) Gray and Petersen
   b) Liddy and Hunt
   c) Magruder and Dean

19. What was the name of the ITT lobbyist who made the mistake of writing a memo outlining a $400,000 contribution by ITT to the Republican Convention in San Diego in return for a "go easy" posture by the Administration toward an illegal ITT merger; who claimed to have a relapse of heart problems upon the memo's being made public; and who was also visited in a Denver hospital by a scruffy fellow in an obviously phony wig (Hunt) who tried to get her to admit the memo was a forgery?

20. Liddy and Dean opposed ITT's proposal to donate $400,000 to the Republican convention site in San Diego. True or false?

21. Fill in the blank in the famous ITT memo: "_____ is definitely helping us, but it cannot be known. Please destroy this, huh?"
   a) Mitchell
   b) Colson
   c) Liddy

22. Who sent Hunt to the Denver hospital?
   a) Colson
   b) He went on his own initiative.
   c) Liddy

23. Where did Hunt get the disguise?
   a) From the Plumbers
   b) From the CIA
   c) His wife made them.

24. What color was Hunt's wig?
    a) Blond
    b) Red
    c) Brown

25. What did Hunt advise Dita Beard to do after she flew back east and told reporters that her ITT memo was a fraud?
    a) Disappear
    b) Feign insanity
    c) Collapse

26. The FBI conducted scientific studies and proved that the Dita Beard memo was a forgery. True or false?

27. What did Colson believe was the White House's primary error in the way it publicly handled the allegations in the ITT matter?
    a) Meeting the allegations head-on
    b) Trying to cover up at an unfortunate time
    c) Allowing Howard Hunt to get involved

28. What members of the Nixon Administration allegedly met with Robert Vesco or his representative and promised to help him buy the U.S. government's interest in a scandal-ridden Lebanese bank?

29. In late 1971, Robert Vesco was jailed in Switzerland at the complaint of an IOS Ltd. mutual-fund investor, but he was freed immediately after a telephone call was made to the U.S. Embassy there, expressing interest in Vesco's jailing. Who was the caller?

30. When questioned about his hiring presidential relative Don Nixon, Vesco replied:
    a) "I like the guy. I think he's got a bright future."
    b) "I'm doing the Nixons a favor. It can't do any harm."
    c) "What's the beef? He'll pull his weight."

31. Ehrlichman said that after March 30, when the President asked him to look into Watergate, he began taping his phone calls to important people, and even did some checking on Haldeman. True or false?

32. How lengthy was the sentence handed down to the Cubans by Judge Sirica on March 23, 1973?
    a) Two and a half years
    b) Forty years
    c) Five years

33. What event could be said to have caused the cover-up to collapse?
    a) The publication of McCord's letter to Judge Sirica
    b) Dean's March 21 "cancer on the presidency" conversation with Nixon
    c) The revelations in the ITT affair

34. To which one of the following men has *not* been attributed the phrase "modified limited hangout"?
    a) Haldeman
    b) Ehrlichman
    c) Mitchell

35. On April 14, just before Hunt testified, Ehrlichman and Haldeman met with Nixon to discuss how to survive Watergate after Hunt's predicted disclosures. What was Haldeman's advice as to "the only way to beat it now"?
    a) Come clean with the public and accept responsibility for bad judgment, but not for criminal acts.
    b) Pin it on Mitchell.
    c) Have Haldeman resign.

36. In accordance with Cover-up Conspiracy Plan Number Three, who did Nixon and Dean decide should disburse the $1 million that Dean estimated would be necessary to hush up the burglars over the next two years?

37. Right after McCord fingered numerous White House aides for complicity in Watergate, who said, "They're trying to hang this on my husband. They're lying from beginning to end"?

38. The owners of the Watergate complex put the following ad in Washington and New York newspapers in the spring of 1973: "Don't be bugged with the commonplace—this spring indulge yourself. Rent an office in the Watergate." True or false?

39. On April 17, 1973, Nixon publicly stated that "real progress" was being made toward finding the truth and that White House staff employees were expected to cooperate fully. How did Ron Ziegler say the press should regard his previous statements on Watergate?
    a) As "essentially truthful"
    b) As "fundamentally uninformed"
    c) As "inoperative"

40. When Dean decided to talk to the federal prosecutors, he told Haldeman, who discouraged him with an analogy to the problem of revealing information and then trying to retrieve it or backtrack. What analogy, which was widely reported, did Haldeman use?

41. When Dean hurriedly spoke to his wife, Mo, to say that he had been fired from his White House job, he told her to remove documents from the attic and to hide others (including the as yet not public Huston plan memorandum) because "they may be coming after it." What scared Mo as much as the dreaded knock on the door?
    a) Finding other "political dynamite" documents
    b) She wasn't sure which documents to burn and which to give to Pat Gray.
    c) Encountering a mouse or a spider

42. In a conversation with Ehrlichman and Haldeman in April 1973, Nixon said, "Give 'em hors d'oeuvre and maybe they won't come back for the main course." Identify (a) the "hors d'oeuvre" and (b) the "main course."

43. Once Nixon knew that Dean had gone to the prosecutors to cut a deal, he fired him immediately. True or false?

44. What was the theme of the Easter Sunday sermon that Nixon heard on the day he learned that Dean had gone to the prosecutors?

45. Nixon issued a statement in late April containing the following words: "Finally, some may hope or think I will become a scape-

goat in the Watergate case. Anyone who believes this does not know me, know the true facts, or understand our system of justice." True or false?

46. Who were "two of the finest public servants it was [Nixon's] privilege to know"?

47. On May 9, 1973, Nixon spoke at a GOP fund-raiser scheduled to raise $2 million. Despite Watergate, he got the $2 million. True or false?

48. When Prosecutor Silbert found out in May 1973 that Petersen, at the Justice Department, had been passing on the results of the grand jury investigation to Nixon, he demanded that Petersen stop and Petersen did. True or false?

49. On May 16, who proposed that Congress create an independent commission to propose ways of reforming the federal election process?
    a) Larry O'Brien
    b) Nixon
    c) Senator Ervin

50. In May 1973, what former cabinet member, amid charges by Republicans that Watergate was giving the party a bad name, made a public display of changing from the Democratic to the Republican party?

51. To what was Democratic leader Rep. Thomas O'Neill referring when he said in May 1973, "First time I ever heard of a rat swimming to a sinking ship"?

52. During the Ellsberg trial, Ehrlichman spoke twice to the presiding judge, Matthew Byrne, about the possibility of Byrne's becoming FBI Director. Ehrlichman was surprised that the press reacted to the overtures to Byrne as an attempt to influence the course of the trial. True or false?

53. The espionage case against Daniel Ellsberg was dismissed in May 1973 on grounds of government misconduct, including not only

the fact that Ellsberg's phone was tapped, but that transcripts of such taping were not presented to the court. The transcripts were never found. True or false?

54. Who stated the following: "It was the system that has brought the facts to light and that will bring those guilty to justice—a system that in this case included . . . a courageous judge, Judge Sirica"?
   a) Senator Ervin
   b) Nixon
   c) A *Washington Post* editorial

Deep Throat Questions

55. Who said the following to whom, and what were the circumstances: "Listen, you son of a bitch, don't you understand the English language? Don't appeal the goddamn case and that's all there is to it"?

56. Why didn't Dean prepare a written report on Watergate, as requested by Haldeman in late March 1973?

57. Who was G. Bradford Cook?

58. Why, in April, before Haldeman and Ehrlichman had resigned, but after Dean had gone to the prosecutors, did Nixon issue the following statement: "I have expressed to the appropriate authorities my views that no individual holding, in the past or present, a position of major importance in the Administration should be given immunity from prosecution"?

59. What did the London *Sunday Times* quote a certain congressman as stating was the reason that Nixon should have had Japanese guards instead of German guards (i.e., Haldeman and Ehrlichman)?

☆6☆

THE PRESS

"One hell of a lot of people don't give one damn about this issue of suppression of the press."
—President Nixon to John Dean, February 18, 1973

"Kicking the press is an art . . . [L]et them have it without rancor. That's what you have to do."
—President Nixon, July 7, 1972

"Don't get the impression you [the press] arouse my anger . . . you see, one can only be angry with those he respects." *—President Nixon, November 17, 1973*

"[A]s far as Watergate is concerned, it has been carried on, it has been, I believe, overpublicized, and a lot of charges have been made that frankly have proved to be false." *—President Nixon, March 15, 1974*

THE TIMES *(November 1972–August 1974)*

Relations between politicians and the press are usually tense. Each needs the other, but each is also sensitive to manipulation.

As the Vietnam controversy got worse, so did government deception. Nixon's always-poor relations with the press became stormy. His apparent unwillingness to do anything about Watergate fueled journalistic fires. Nixon had previously loosed Agnew to attack an "effete corps of impudent snobs" and brought the power of the presidency into the struggle by commandeering federal agencies to lean on the media. Hunt and Liddy were just barely restrained.

Nixon truly believed the press was out to get him. "[They] hate me because I have beaten them so often. . . . The only time they are nice to you is when they think you are finished."

After the 1972 election, both sides took off the gloves.

QUESTIONS

1. Which White House official penned the following in a 1970 memo to Magruder on the subject of monitoring the press: "I'll approve whatever will work—and am concerned with results—not methods"?
   a) Haldeman
   b) Nixon
   c) Dean

2. In a 1969 memo to the President from Jeb Magruder concerning unfavorable press coverage, Magruder suggested that "shotgunning" was not the best way "to get the media." What did he suggest?
   a) The President should set forth his objections in a slanted "white paper."
   b) Harassment of the press by the IRS and the antitrust division of the Justice Department.
   c) Call for a public Senate investigation.

3. Nixon did not blame the press for the unfavorable coverage of Watergate. True or false?

4. Nixon believed that the press wrote about White House slush funds simply because the press hated Nixon. True or false?

5. Nixon once suggested that the press would never have played up Watergate if:
   a) He had not had the 1960 election stolen from him by Mayor Daley.
   b) He had been a liberal and bugged out of Vietnam.
   c) He had been a Jew who had been on the *Harvard Crimson.*

6. Which of the three TV networks devoted the most time to Watergate between Labor Day and the election?
   a) ABC
   b) CBS
   c) NBC

7. Of the approximately 1,200 domestic full-time correspondents in Washington, how many worked full-time on the Watergate story before Election Day 1972?
   a) Fewer than twenty
   b) About fifty
   c) Almost two hundred

8. Of the 1,400 daily newspapers that endorsed candidates for the presidency in 1972, more than 90 percent endorsed Nixon. True or false?

9. Ziegler once described his job to a Senate press secretary as:
   a) "Downfield blocking."
   b) "Fronting for the President."
   c) "Lying to reporters."

10. Who said, "Ron [Ziegler] is the best press secretary in history; the members of the press corps tell me so"?
    a) Nixon
    b) Kissinger
    c) Ehrlichman

11. When Ziegler requested the necessary information from Dean to answer pointed and repeated questions about Watergate, Dean told him nothing. True or false?

12. When *The New York Times* reported Nixon's pardon of two previously convicted members of the very accounting firm that had
audited Nixon's questionable personal finances, how did Ziegler
characterize the story?
a) False
b) Silly
c) Not newsworthy

13. On May 22, 1973, Garment, Buzhardt, and Ziegler held a press
briefing concerning a 4,000-word public statement by Nixon,
which, among other things, admitted his initial approval of the
Huston plan. In that connection, the following question was
asked:

> "Based on this briefing alone, I come away with the im-
> pression that the President engaged in a conspiracy to com-
> mit an illegal act; that is, the evidence is here on the top of
> page three that the President approved an illegal act. Now
> there has not been any statement . . . to counter that suspi-
> cion and I am wondering if you can clear it up?"

Which of the three Nixon men made the following response:

> "First of all, there was no act. Second of all, the President
> did not engage in a conspiracy, as he clearly states in both
> statements, and there you have a specific comment in rela-
> tion to that assertion."

a) Garment
b) Buzhardt
c) Ziegler

14. What was the substance of a phony internal memorandum—written by Haldeman in 1973 to be leaked to the press—that would
show Nixon's restraint and fair play during the 1972 campaign?
a) The FBI had dossiers on certain high-level McGovern staffers,
demonstrating a connection with foreign governments.
b) CREEP had concrete evidence of dirty tricks by McGovern
staffers, but because of Segretti's unauthorized excesses, Nixon
had decided not to publicize the information.
c) McGovern had fathered an illegitimate child in the 1940s.

16.   17.   18.

19.   20.   21.

22.   23.   24.

Photo I.D. Quiz #3

15. Nixon went so far as to ban even selected society reporters from White House functions. True or false?

16. Deputy Attorney General Ruckelshaus found records of wiretaps of news reporters in a White House safe. True or false?

17. Nixon released the names of other individuals taped by previous administrations. True or false?

18. Nixon suggested wiretapping *The New York Times.* True or false?

19. Which one of the following was *not* the substance of a phony phone call received by CBS?
    a) A caller who identified himself as Gary Hart suggested that CBS not play up the Watergate break-in since McGovern supporters had staged a few break-ins of their own.
    b) A caller who identified himself as Frank Mankiewicz suggested that CBS should disregard their previous deal to give 80 percent of the news coverage to McGovern and only 20 percent to Nixon, and should now give Nixon more.
    c) A caller who identified himself as McGovern's TV expert stated falsely that McGovern had canceled his TV speech calling for an end to the Vietnam War.

20. To what reporter did Ehrlichman actually say the following: "I think you're slanted. I don't know whether it's just sloppiness or you're letting your true feelings come through, but the net effect is that you're negative. You have negative leads on bad stories"?

21. A television news story alleged that Bebe Rebozo was the administrator of a secret $1 million fund for Nixon's private use. When Nixon attacked the story, who was the commentator he was referring to by the following: "When a commentator takes a bit of news and then, with knowledge of what the facts are, distorts it viciously, I have no respect for that individual"?

22. In referring to the Nixon-oriented attacks on the press as Watergate unfolded, what TV commentator said: "What I object to in criticism from the White House is not in fact that there is criticism, not even the fact that they would try to raise their credibility by attacking [the press's]. . . . But what has happened is

that this Administration, throughout what I believe to be a considered and concerted campaign, has managed to politicize the issue of the press versus the Administration to the point that now [the press] . . . come[s] to the real crunch, which is the matter of [its] . . . actual freedom to operate, [its] . . . freedom to criticize, [its] . . . right to do that"?

23. Aside from locker-room talk and threats, did any of *The Washington Post* Company's television station licenses ever get challenged?

24. What did Colson say to the presidents of the three major TV networks about equal time for opposition statements after Nixon prime-time broadcasts?
    a) The White House would selectively limit access to the President by any network that gave equal time to opposition statements.
    b) It was not required under law and should not be permitted, and the White House would petition the FCC to enjoin the networks from airing equal-time responses.
    c) The White House would try to strip the networks of certain wholly-owned TV stations.

25. Among Hunt, Liddy, and Colson, numerous schemes were proposed to "take care of" syndicated columnist Jack Anderson. Which one of the following was *not* one of their schemes?
    a) Putting LSD on his car's steering wheel
    b) Staging an automobile accident
    c) Poisoning his aspirin
    d) Staging a street crime
    e) Putting a rabid dog in his house
    f) Feeding him LSD before he went on television

Deep Throat Questions
26. What famous political advisor once said the following: "You don't answer anything until you are convinced that the opposition has completely saturated the field on the subject. . . . When you answer it, do so with any attack of your own against the opposition for having launched it in the first place"?

27. Who was Ms. Patricia O'Leary?

THE SATURDAY NIGHT MASSACRE

"As I have said before and I have said throughout this entire matter, all government employees and especially White House staff employees are expected fully to cooperate in this matter. I condemn any attempts to cover up in this case no matter who is involved."

—*President Nixon, April 17, 1973*

"Let others wallow in Watergate. We're going to do our job." —*President Nixon, July 20, 1973*

"I was elected to do a job. Watergate is an episode that I deeply deplore; and, had I been running the campaign—rather than trying to run the country . . . it would never have happened."

—*President Nixon, August 22, 1973*

"The pall of Watergate, with its revelations of misplaced loyalties, of strange measures of the unethical, of unusual doings in high places, and by lawyer after lawyer, is upon us . . . [such that the] very glue of our ship of state seems about to come unstuck."

—*Supreme Court Justice Harry Blackmun, August 1973*

"I have a quality which—I guess I must have inherited it from my midwestern mother and father—which is that the tougher it gets, the cooler I get."

—*President Nixon, October 26, 1973*

THE TIMES *(Summer–Fall 1973)*

In the winter of 1973, Haldeman, Ehrlichman, Dean, and Moore met in La Costa, California, to develop a strategy for taking on the Ervin committee. They decided to make a public display of cooperation but in truth to make access to witnesses and information as difficult as they could. They decided further to discredit the Democrats publicly (by showing that they too engaged in dirty tricks) and to conduct a behind-the-scenes media effort to stamp the Ervin committee as partisan.

The Nixon attacks were virulent. Ziegler attacked "irresponsible leaks of tidal-wave proportions," but could not stem the rising tide of profound suspicion that grew as one Nixon official after another testified to shabby behavior or offered perjury or half-truth. Modern mass theater (TV) beamed the depth of wrongdoing into every American home.

Public opinion was profoundly altered. Even the apparently trusting Henry Petersen seemed to speak for the entire public when he said, "They don't act like innocent people."

In May 1973, the new Attorney General, Elliot Richardson, appointed his old law professor, former Solicitor General Archibald Cox, as Special Prosecutor to investigate Watergate-related crimes. Cox agreed to take the job only upon an express guarantee of independence from Richardson.

Dean's riveting testimony occurred in late June and was highlighted by his descriptions of the March 21 "cancer on the presidency" meeting with Nixon. Yet, even after Dean's testimony in the summer of 1973, the Special Prosecutor did not have enough evidence. Haldeman, Ehrlichman, and Mitchell would not say a thing. Dean clammed up without a guarantee of immunity. The White House refused to produce any documentary evidence.

The logjam was shattered by the revelation that Nixon had been taping his Oval Office conversations for years. Immediately the Ervin committee and the Special Prosecutor filed requests for the tapes of key Watergate conversations.

All summer, while the Ervin committee hearings dragged on, Nixon resisted every attempt to part with the tapes. He refused all compromises and stated that he had listened to the tapes and that they supported his version of the Watergate events.

While Cox pressed for the tapes, he also probed numerous other areas that were highly sensitive and damaging to the President. He investigated the wiretaps that had been placed on government officials and newscasters under a flimsy national security blanket, the 1970 Town House Operation, the rough handling of anti-Nixon demonstrators during the 1972 campaign, the activities of the Plumbers, and Nixon's personal finances.

Cox finally petitioned the court for enforcement of his request for the tapes. Judge Sirica ordered the President to comply. Upon appeal of the order, the court of appeals upheld Judge Sirica's order. Nixon was in a box.

Determined not to surrender the tapes, Nixon on October 20, 1973, dismissed Cox and accepted the resignations of Attorney General Richardson and Deputy Attorney General William Ruckelshaus.

The American public was incensed. A "firestorm," General Haig termed the reaction to the Saturday Night Massacre. Nixon finally backed down, released the tapes, and agreed to appoint a new Special Prosecutor.

QUESTIONS

1. What prominent Democratic politician was Nixon convinced was behind the Senate Watergate Committee organization and hearings?
   a) Teddy Kennedy
   b) Larry O'Brien
   c) George McGovern

2. How many communications did the Ervin committee receive from interested private citizens concerning the investigation?
   a) More than 1 million
   b) Just under 500,000
   c) Just over 100,000

3. Before the Senate Watergate Committee began its investigations, Senator Ervin already believed Nixon was involved in the cover-up. True or false?

4. Not surprisingly, the vote in the Senate to establish the Ervin committee was close and divided along party lines. True or false?

5. Erle Stanley Gardner once asked Sam Dash, counsel to the Senate Watergate Committee, to join the staff of mystery writers who fleshed out the outlines of his detective-novel plots. True or false?

6. Just after the Watergate Committee was organized, what position did Nixon take respecting the testimony of his aides and former aides?

7. Who publicly called the Ervin hearings a "rain dance" and a "beauty contest" with a "Perry Masonish impact"?
   a) Vice President Agnew
   b) Secretary of Agriculture Earl Butz
   c) Sen. William Saxbe

8. What member of the Nixon Administration (who once said the Pope should disqualify himself from opining on birth control on the grounds that "He no playa da game, he no makea da rules") called the Ervin committee a "very improper political inquisition"?
   a) Vice President Agnew
   b) Secretary of Agriculture Earl Butz
   c) Sen. William Saxbe

9. What individual, who once said that Nixon appeared to have "left his senses" by resuming bombing in Vietnam, and who called Haldeman and Ehrlichman "Nazis," nonetheless also referred to the Ervin hearings as a "kangaroo court," a "rump court," and a "Roman holiday"?
   a) Vice President Agnew
   b) Secretary of Agriculture Earl Butz
   c) Sen. William Saxbe

10. Did Senator Ervin deny the validity of the concept of executive privilege in the U.S. Constitution?

11. The Ervin committee heard thirty-seven witnesses in thirty-five days. Which one of the following major Nixon Administration figures did *not* testify?
    a) Ehrlichman
    b) Colson
    c) Chapin

12. Senator Ervin objected to Haldeman's (a private citizen) listening
to the tapes of the famous September 15 and March 21 meetings
with Dean and the President and then testifying about them as if
from memory. In this connection, match the following Ervin
phrases with their meanings.

a) "Colludin' together" 1) Haldeman's statement that he only
testified about what he had heard on
the tapes after the Ervin committee
had overruled his objections that,
because of a presidential order, he
could not discuss what he heard on
the tapes.

b) "Counterfeit 2) The fact that John Wilson, Halde-
evidence" man's lawyer, had checked with the
White House before Haldeman prepared a written amendment to his
statement concerning the March 21
meeting.

c) "Powder-puff 3) The fact that Haldeman had heard
objection" the tapes and the Ervin committee
had not.

13. About what witness did Sam Ervin make the following observation: "An honest man is the noblest work of God"?
a) Hugh Sloan
b) Ehrlichman
c) Magruder

14. In view of his vague responses before the Judiciary Committee,
what did Senator Ervin tell witness Kleindienst was even "better
than a good memory"?

15. Dean didn't receive immunity for his testimony before the Ervin
committee. True or false?

16. As part of an effort to discredit Dean, the White House leaked a
story that Dean bargained for immunity because he was afraid of
being sent to jail. Why?

17. The highlight of Dean's statement to the committee focused on
the notebooks he had taken from Hunt's safe. True or false?

18. Why did Woodward and Bernstein suggest that Dean should put all he knew about Watergate on tape and give it to them?
    a) There were rumors that Dean's life was threatened.
    b) Bernstein and Woodward were required by *The Washington Post* to have two sources for every fact.
    c) They wanted an exclusive story, and they knew that once Dean began talking to the prosecutors, the information would come out anyway.

19. Haldeman wrote a memorandum dated February 9, 1973, which suggested that the White House order the chairman of PepsiCo to fire a former FBI agent then working for PepsiCo, because he would not tell the White House about the FBI's wiretapping of Nixon during the 1968 campaign. When Senator Weicker saw the memo, he said, "Oh, I see, we now have the White House reaching down through you and saying to citizens of this country, if they don't do what is asked of them, they will be fired." Did Haldeman dispute Weicker's interpretation of the memo?

20. What did one of Senator Inouye's staff suggest that the senator tell reporters he had actually said when, during Ehrlichman's testimony, Inouye was heard to have remarked into a live microphone, "What a liar"?

21. When Liddy told his secretary, Sally Harmony, that he would be involved in clandestine activities, she asked him never to let her know because she preferred being ignorant. True or false?

22. What was Liddy's response when Senator Ervin asked him, "Do you solemnly swear to tell the truth, the whole truth and nothing but the truth, so help you God?"

23. Whom did White House aide Richard Moore quote to the committee as saying to him, "I have racked my brain. I have searched my mind. Were there any clues I should have seen that should have tipped me off?"
    a) Assistant Attorney General Henry Petersen
    b) Prosecutor Earl Silbert
    c) Nixon
    d) Haldeman
    e) James St. Clair

24. Who told the committee the following: "In the service of my country I withstood hours and hours of depth-charging, shelling, bombing, but I never expected to run into a Watergate in the service of the President of the United States"?
    a) Hunt
    b) Liddy
    c) Gray

25. Who made the following comment: "I cannot escape feeling that the country I have served for my entire life and which directed me to carry out the Watergate entry is punishing me for doing the very things it trained and directed me to do"?
    a) Hunt
    b) Liddy
    c) Gray

26. What member of the Ervin committee visited the Cubans in Danbury prison at their request and, despite telling them that he had "no influence at the White House," was told by Martinez, "Ah, Senator, we watched you on television. We wanted to talk to you because you would understand us. You are the only romantic on the committee!"?

27. Who was the first President to install taping equipment in the Oval Office?
    a) Nixon
    b) John Kennedy
    c) Franklin Roosevelt

28. Dean was the first person who suggested to the Senate Watergate Committee staff that Nixon had a taping system in his office. True or false?

29. Dean welcomed the revelation of the presidential taping system. True or false?

30. Which of the following men did *not* know about the presidential taping system?
    a) Nixon
    b) Haldeman
    c) Ehrlichman
    d) Butterfield
    e) Higby
    f) Certain Secret Service members

31. Who made the following comment: "I would not like to be a Russian leader. They never know when they're being taped"?

32. What other major figure in the Watergate drama also recorded his telephone calls?
    a) Dean
    b) Liddy
    c) Special Prosecutor Cox

33. It has been reported that some Nixon aides taped their telephone conversations with Nixon after Watergate, but none taped their conversations before Watergate. True or false?

34. Nixon publicly accused Presidents Kennedy and Johnson of large-scale burglarizing without court orders. True or false?

35. Which *two* of the following suggested to Nixon that he destroy the tapes?
    a) Buzhardt   d) Pat Nixon
    b) Haig   e) Len Garment
    c) Buchanan

36. Who thought the taping was really crazy and said, "To leave yourself to the mercy of historians like that is unbelievable irresponsibility"?

37. Even as late as August 1973, most Americans felt that the drowning of Mary Jo Kopechne was more "morally reprehensible" than the Watergate bugging. True or false?

38. Despite Watergate, the Oliver Quale poll of late August 1973 showed that Nixon would win a rerun of the 1972 presidential election if it were held at that time. True or false?

39. When Elliot Richardson became the new Attorney General, Nixon told him to pursue the investigation even if it led to the President. True or false?

40. Nixon promised not to invoke executive privilege in regard to any testimony concerning possible criminal conduct. True or false?

41. The Federal Immunity Statute, which allowed the Special Prosecutor to pierce the cover-up, was drafted under which President?

42. What was the first reaction of the Special Prosecutor's Office to the revelation of the presidential taping system?
    a) Unrestrained enthusiasm
    b) Rank disbelief
    c) Fear of a Nixonian ruse

43. What did Liddy tell the Special Prosecutor was the most subversive thing to happen to the country during this century?
    a) The Plumbers' break-in
    b) The investigation of Watergate offenses
    c) The presence of KGB agents in the DNC

44. Despite the President's intransigence about releasing the tapes, did Cox ever suggest that he might press to have the President held in contempt?

45. What did the White House (in the words of Elliot Richardson) regard as a "ravenous beast with an insatiable appetite"?
    a) The press
    b) The outraged American public
    c) Archibald Cox's office

46. In connection with the "Stennis compromise" suggested by Nixon (wherein Senator Stennis of Mississippi would listen to the nine subpoenaed tapes and verify the relevancy and accuracy of transcripts to be given to Cox instead of the tapes), Senator Stennis's acute hearing made him the obvious choice. True or false?

47. Senator Stennis agreed to the "transcript submission" compromise concerning the tapes. True or false?

48. Neither Baker, Ervin, nor Richardson agreed to the "Stennis compromise." True or false?

49. What important political figure did Nixon tell Richardson would not understand if he did not fire Cox?

50. The prosecutors hid copies of key documents right before Cox was fired. True or false?

51. Immediately after the firing of Cox, FBI agents showed up at the Special Prosecutor's Office to lock the prosecutors out of their offices. True or false?

52. Nixon expected the adverse public reaction to the firing of Cox. True or false?

53. How did presidential aide Richard Moore describe Nixon's firing of Cox to the press?
    a) "His greatest coup"
    b) "An unfortunate inevitability"
    c) "Provoked and well-earned by Cox"

54. What significant international action did Nixon take five days after the Saturday Night Massacre?

Deep Throat Questions
55. To what was Nixon referring when he made the following remark concerning the tapes: "If Lipshits gets off with copping a plea . . . and getting a suspended sentence . . . what in the name of Christ is this all about?"

56. What phrase did Senator Ervin use to characterize unchecked executive privilege as seen by Nixon?

57. How did the new Attorney General phrase his disbelief concerning White House assertions that it was not aware of activities by Segretti, Liddy, and others?

58. Why did Nixon privately call Agnew his "insurance policy"?

59. What did Frank Mankiewicz tell the Ervin committee would be "the final Watergate dirty trick [to] have been played—on all of us"?

60. Who was Harry Toulmin?

☆8☆

THE TAPES

"And in the months ahead, I shall do everything that I can to see that any doubts as to the integrity of the man who occupies the highest office in this land—and to remove those doubts where they existed."
                              —President Nixon, November 7, 1973

"I am sure that you have read the charge, and you have heard it, that I, Senator Nixon, took $18,000 from a group of my supporters. . . . Let me say this: not one cent of the $18,000 went to Senator Nixon for my personal use." *—President Nixon, September 23, 1952,*
                              in the "Checkers speech"

"I made my mistakes but in all my years of public life, I have never profited from public service. I have earned every cent. Well, I am not a crook, I have earned everything I have got." *—President Nixon, November 17, 1981*

"The theory that there has been a conscious effort to conceal evidence is no longer a theory."
                              —Rep. John B. Anderson

THE TIMES *(Fall 1973)*

The release of the tapes began an unending series of disastrous revelations; falling "bombshells" kept Watergate on the front page all fall and winter. Highlights included missing tapes, gaps in tapes, embarrassing courtroom hearings focusing on tampering with the tapes, new revelations concerning the ITT matter and the President's personal taxes, the repudiation by former Plumber Egil Krogh of Nixon's "national security" defense, and further disclosures concerning the milk-price scandal.

Late in the fall, Nixon promised a crowd in Memphis "no more bombshells." The very next day an 18½-minute gap was found in a critical segment of one of the subpoenaed tapes. Several days later, in reaction to questions about his personal finances, Nixon asserted that he was "not a crook."

The Ervin committee conducted further public hearings focused on "dirty tricks," and the House Judiciary Committee took up the question of impeachment. Nixon retained criminal attorney James St. Clair.

From Nixon's viewpoint, the new Special Prosecutor, Leon Jaworski, was no improvement over Archibald Cox; Jaworski subpoenaed tapes by the bucketful. Nixon was determined to resist. Once again the Special Prosecutor went into federal court to compel the President to relinquish the tapes.

QUESTIONS

1. Just after the dismissal of Cox, Nixon announced that Senator Ervin had approved Nixon's offer to provide transcripts to the Special Prosecutor in lieu of the actual tapes. Nixon's announcement was the first Ervin had heard of the offer. True or false?

2. Which one of the following images was *not* part of Nixon's autumn public-relations counterattack?
   a) Nixon as detective, ferreting out the truth to see justice done
   b) Nixon accepting responsibility and shaking up the government
   c) Nixon wrapping himself in the "national security" issue
   d) Nixon moving to show that he had opened his Administration to Congress and the public

e) Nixon accepting the blame for, and working hard to correct, campaign abuses

f) Nixon showing his preoccupation with the government's business while letting others "wallow in Watergate"

g) Nixon showing himself as harassed and abused by the media

h) Nixon again showing his preoccupation with government business and "doing something" to demonstrate his indispensability

i) Nixon opening himself to the courts and Congress (though only partially) through "Operation Candor"

3. Despite his poor reputation for withholding subpoenaed tapes, Nixon refused to offer even non-subpoenaed tapes to the Special Prosecutor. True or false?

4. Presidential counsel Buzhardt initially told Judge Sirica that two conversations had not been recorded on the nine tapes subpoenaed by Special Prosecutor Cox. As these conversations were unrelated to Watergate, they didn't matter. True or false?

5. Presidential counsel Buzhardt also told Judge Sirica that there were other blanks in the remaining subpoenaed tapes. How many did he say contained blanks?
   a) A few
   b) A lot
   c) All

6. Because of the strictly monitored system for withdrawing tapes from the tape depository in the White House, it was easy to determine who had been listening to Watergate tapes, and when. True or false?

7. The President maintained a separate log of his activities until his resignation. True or false?

8. There were no gaps in the President's Dictabelt recordings. True or false?

9. What did Ehrlichman testify that he and the President had discussed at the meeting on June 20 (three days after the break-in)

for one hour and nineteen minutes—the tape of which meeting now had the 18½-minute gap?
   a) Public-relations implications in Watergate
   b) Welfare reform and busing
   c) Plumber's activities

10. No one can ever be sure that the 18½-minute gap wiped out a Watergate discussion. True or false?

11. The first time Rose Mary Woods testified before Judge Sirica, she denied that she could have caused a tape erasure. True or false?

12. After Rose Mary Woods testified about the erasure on the June 20, 1972, tape, Jaworski suggested that the originals of the tapes be placed in Judge Sirica's custody "so that there couldn't be anything happening to them." The White House said the idea was nonsense. True or false?

13. What was the "Rose Mary stretch"?

14. How did Rose Mary Woods duplicate the "Rose Mary stretch" in the courtroom?

15. What was the finding of the tape experts as to the explanation for the 18½-minute gap?
   a) Unexplained
   b) Deliberate erasure
   c) A faulty tape recorder

16. Presidential counsel Buzhardt thought Rose Mary Woods had erased the tape. True or false?

17. Haig thought Nixon erased the tape. True or false?

18. According to the designer of the tape system, why did the tape of the April 15 meeting with Dean run out?
   a) Nixon talked too much.
   b) Butterfield forgot to load the machine.
   c) A television had been brought into the Oval Office; the non-stop noise kept the voice-activated tape running.

19. What was the significance of the fact that the tape box containing the April 15 tape was marked "Part 1"?

20. There wasn't any evidence that anyone had listened to the important April 15 tape. True or false?

21. Why didn't the Special Prosecutor subpoena the Dictabelt containing Nixon's own recollections of the April 15, 1973, meeting with Dean?
    a) He was told by the White House that the Dictabelt was missing.
    b) He did not know it existed.
    c) He assumed the recollections would be self-serving.

22. In view of the fact that the tape for the April 15 meeting was missing and the Dictabelt for the same day could not be found, what did Nixon suggest to his counsel?
    a) That he manufacture a new Dictabelt and pass it off as the original
    b) That he claim that he just hadn't had the time to use the Dictabelt that day
    c) That he claim that there was no Dictabelt used that day because Dictabelt recordings were only made for foreign-policy recollections

23. What was presidential counsel Buzhardt's explanation for gaps in the President's Dictabelt of the March 21 "cancer on the presidency" meeting with Dean?
    a) The President was clumsy.
    b) The tape was faulty.
    c) The President purposely turned off the system.

24. On September 10, 1973, Sen. Howard Baker said "I have an idea the greatest crisis the country faced has passed on Watergate." Baker reaffirmed this statement even two months later. True or false?

25. What did Senator Baker mean when he said, on ABC's "Issues and Answers," "There are animals crashing around in the forest. I can hear them, but I can't see them"?

26. On November 17, 1973, Nixon was asked what his plans were when he left the White House, and he replied that it depended on when he left. True or false?

27. What was the President's name for his new public-relations offensive, which he launched in a speech to Republican governors in November?

28. In 1969, a friend of Nixon's loaned him $625,000 to help buy the San Clemente property. In 1970 this same friend formed an investment company to buy back the property, minus 5.9 acres containing the house, for $1,249,000 plus cancellation of the original $625,000 loan. Who was Nixon's friend?

29. Which of the following "improvements" to Nixon's residences at San Clemente and Key Biscayne did the U.S. government *not* pay for?
    a) Weed removal
    b) Furnishings for Nixon's den
    c) A doghouse for King Timahoe
    d) A new heating system
    e) Flagpoles

30. On May 24, White House deputy press secretary Gerald Warren issued a statement saying that the U.S. government had spent $39,000 on improvements to the Nixon property. On May 28, UPI put the figure at more than $100,000. Which was the truer figure?

31. What was the "presidential papers caper"?
    a) Nixon backdated the date on a deed of donation to get a huge tax deduction.
    b) Numerous CREEP financial documents subpoenaed by the Special Prosecutor could not be found.
    c) The altered tape transcripts.

32. Why did Nixon suggest that his vice-presidential papers were worth $500,000?
    a) The information was rather revealing.
    b) He was an active Vice President.
    c) Humphrey got a lot for his.

33. Nixon announced to the press, "I am not a crook." Match the following similar statements by other Nixon Administration officials with the speaker:
    a) "I am not a whore."   1) Vice President Agnew
    b) "I've never stolen   2) Assistant Attorney
       any money."   General Henry
                                     Petersen
    c) "I have nothing to hide." 3) John Mitchell

34. Where was the press conference held when Nixon said "I am not a crook"?
    a) The Oval Office
    b) San Clemente
    c) Fantasyland, Walt Disney World

35. Upon leaving the "I am not a crook" press conference, what did Nixon ask a man and a boy outside the area?
    a) He asked if he was a crook.
    b) He asked if he was the boy's mother or grandmother.
    c) He asked if they didn't think the press had become preoccupied with Watergate and that perhaps, in view of the world situation, foreign-policy formulation might be a more productive area of inquiry.

36. Kissinger suggested that Nixon apologize publicly. What was Ziegler's reaction?
    a) "We could all use fresh air."
    b) "It would be an important gesture by a great man."
    c) "Contrition is bullshit."
    d) "Fire Kissinger."

37. What familiar question did Sen. Barry Goldwater raise publicly in a December 17 interview concerning Nixon's reputation for honesty?

Deep Throat Questions
38. How many private offices did Nixon have, and how many of them were equipped with sophisticated communications equipment?

39. What was the "Slippery Gulch Rodeo"?

☆9☆

THE END

"There is a time to be timid. There is a time to be conciliatory. There is a time to fly and there is a time to fight. And I'm going to fight like hell."
—*President Nixon, January 22, 1974*

"One year of Watergate is enough."
—*President Nixon, January 30, 1974*

"Why doesn't the President resign? Because if the President resigned when he was not guilty of charges, then every President in the future could be forced out of office by simply leveling the charges and getting the media to carry them, and getting a few congressmen and senators who were on the other side to exploit them."
—*President Nixon, March 15, 1974*

"Dragging out Watergate drags down America."
—*President Nixon, May 19, 1974*

"I pray we did the right thing [in voting an impeachment article]. I hoped it didn't have to be this way."
—*Peter Rodino, chairman,*
House Judiciary Committee, July 27, 1974

"[I]t has become evident to me that I no longer have a strong enough political base in the Congress to justify continuing. . . ."   —*President Nixon, August 8, 1974*

THE TIMES *(Spring–Summer 1974)*

By spring 1974, one after another of the nation's most conservative legislators had abandoned ship. Most Americans had ceased to believe the President.

Jaworski continued to press for the tapes because he needed them to prosecute other Watergate defendants. On March 1, the Special Prosecutor announced indictments of Haldeman, Ehrlichman, Mitchell, Colson, Mardian, Parkinson, and Strachan for participation in the cover-up and other crimes. Jaworski kept secret the fact that the grand jury had wished to indict the President but had agreed instead to list him as an unindicted co-conspirator.

As the President continued twisting and turning to avoid releasing the tapes, all other compromises failed. On April 30 he released his own transcribed versions of the tapes in a last-ditch effort to satisfy the clamor.

The American public was shocked at the shabby behavior even in the sanitized transcripts. Public debate shifted from appraising "degree of culpability" to defining an "impeachable offense."

Neither Jaworski nor the House Judiciary Committee, which held closed sessions on the question of impeachment throughout May and June, would accept the transcripts in lieu of the tapes.

Summer 1974 witnessed another riveting display of mass public theater as the members of the House Judiciary Committee, particularly Southern Democrats and Republicans, reluctantly bent to the overwhelming evidence of presidential misconduct and recommended articles of impeachment for obstruction of justice, abuse of power, and contempt of Congress.

The Ervin committee filed its report finding widespread campaign violations. But the real drama lay with the Supreme Court, which was presented with the question of whether the U.S. courts could compel the President to release the tapes. Lurking in the background was the fear that Nixon might disregard such an order anyway.

The Supreme Court decided against the President, and he obeyed the order. Nixon aides knew the President was finished the moment they heard a tape of a Nixon-Haldeman conversation of June 23, 1972, six days after the break-in, which revealed Nixon's participation in the cover-up. The President had not allowed his counsel to hear the tape until the Supreme Court decision. The tape proved to be the "smoking gun." Within days the President resigned.

QUESTIONS

1. In spring 1974, Alexander Haig assigned the responsibility for a new public-relations effort beyond "Operation Candor" to the author of the "Canuck letter." True or false?

2. Senate Minority Leader Hugh Scott told the press that he wouldn't "be a goddamn patsy." He claimed that he had been shown unpublished White House transcripts of tapes indicating that Nixon had no knowledge of the cover-up until he met with Dean on March 21, and that those transcripts "entirely exculpated" the President. Was Scott in fact a "patsy"?

3. Robert Strauss, Chairman of the Democratic National Committee, called for Nixon's resignation as early as January 1974. True or false?

4. What did unflagging Nixon supporter Rabbi Korff say to John Herbert after his article on Korff and the grass-roots pro-Nixon movement championed by him was published?

5. What did White House reporters jokingly suggest was the best way to get an appointment with the President?
   a) Indicate that you were a "sinister force."
   b) Circulate a petition to take out a newspaper ad in Nixon's behalf.
   c) Say you represented major-league baseball and thought he might be interested in being a commissioner.

6. In March 1974, McCord charged that Nixon committed a crime by failing to report what he knew about hush money to law-enforcement authorities. What was St. Clair's response to that charge?
   a) It was not a crime.
   b) Nixon didn't have to, because he was the nation's chief law-enforcement officer.
   c) McCord was a convicted felon.

7. To what was Nixon referring when he said, "The materials I make public tomorrow will provide all the additional evidence needed to get Watergate behind us, and get it behind us now"?

8. What legal victory encouraged Nixon to release the transcripts?

9. Whom did the press play up as the key prosecution witness in that case?

10. Which one of the following men most feared the release of the transcripts?
    a) Ziegler
    b) Haig
    c) Buzhardt

11. During his address to the nation on April 29, 1974, the day he released the transcripts of the tapes, Nixon stated, "I shall invite Chairman Rodino and the committee's ranking minority member, Congressman Hutchinson of Michigan, to come to the White House and listen to the actual full tapes of the conversations so that they can determine for themselves beyond question that the transcripts are accurate and that everything on the tapes relevant to my knowledge and my actions on Watergate is included." Did Nixon ever actually extend such an invitation?

12. The transcripts released by the White House on April 30, 1974, contained the same version of the tapes as the versions given by the White House to the Special Prosecutor in January 1974 and to the Judiciary Committee in March 1974. True or false?

13. How did Ziegler justify the fact that the White House transcripts left out the Nixon statement: "I want you all to stonewall it, let them plead the Fifth Amendment, cover up, or anything else"?
    a) "Of dubious relevance"
    b) "Not Watergate-related"
    c) "Mere locker-room talk"

14. How did Gerald Ford react to the transcripts?
    a) He claimed that Nixon was innocent.
    b) He claimed that Nixon was guilty.
    c) He was appalled at the language.

15. Administration officials were privately aghast at Nixon's perform-
ance on the tapes, but Father John McLaughlin, Jesuit priest and
special assistant to the President, went public to describe his disappointment. True or false?

16. Who once criticized Harry Truman, saying, "I can only say that
I'm very proud that President Eisenhower restored the dignity
and, frankly, good language to the conduct of the presidency of
the United States."
    a) Nixon
    b) Barry Goldwater
    c) Former presidential candidate Thomas Dewey

17. Nixon called Sirica a "goddamn wop" on the tapes. True or false?

18. The Judiciary Committee's version of a March 13, 1973, conversation among the President, Dean, and Haldeman showed the
President and Dean discussing the intelligence-gathering operation at CREEP. When Dean at first said that he did not think that
Mitchell knew of the operation, the President said, "You kid-
ding?" Did the White House transcript of this portion of the conversation contain the President's response?

19. The Judiciary Committee's version of a conversation among
Nixon, Dean, Haldeman, Ehrlichman, and Mitchell on March
22, 1973, has the President saying, ". . . put the fires out almost
got the damn thing nailed down till past the election and so forth.
We all know what it is. Embarrassing goddamn thing the way it
went, and so forth. But, in my view, ah, some of it will come out;
we will survive it. That's the way it is. That's the way you've got to
look at it." The White House version of this portion of the conversation reported Nixon's statement almost verbatim. True or
false?

20. The Judiciary Committee's version of a conversation among
Nixon, Dean, Ehrlichman, and Haldeman on March 21, 1973,
has the President saying, "I ask for a, a written report, which I
think uh, that—which is very general, understand. Understand,
[laughs] I don't want to get all that goddamned specific. I'm
thinking now in far more general terms. . . ." The White House

version of this portion of the conversation reported the President's statement about not wanting to be specific. True or false?

21. To highlight his disgust at Watergate, with what early political document did Rep. William Cohen, a Judiciary Committee member, contrast the Nixon transcripts?
    a) *The Federalist Papers*
    b) Treaties with the Indians
    c) *Pilgrim's Progress*

22. After release of the transcripts, what close Nixon supporter suggested that Nixon plead *nolo contendere* and admit serious (but not criminal) misjudgment?
    a) J. Fred Buzhardt
    b) Spiro Agnew
    c) David Eisenhower

23. Who was the chief architect of Nixon's defense strategy vis-à-vis the impeachment inquiry?

24. What liberal Jew, who once played jazz clarinet in Woody Herman's band, was a loyal friend and confidant to Nixon and became one of his closest advisors during the last year of Watergate?

25. Rep. Paul McCloskey, who ran against Nixon in 1972, said that Nixon was probably "scared to death to resign because he knows he could go to jail. If I were his lawyer I'd be urging him not to resign. The trouble is that there's nobody to plea-bargain with the President, as they did with Vice President Agnew. The Justice Department can't do it; they work for him [Nixon]." How did McCloskey propose to get around this problem?

26. What was the "Russian roulette" compromise proposed by Haig to Rep. Barber Conable?

27. Why was St. Clair willing to consider a compromise with Jaworski with respect to surrendering the subpoenaed tapes, even though Nixon had instructed him never even to consider it?

28. Nixon never said that he would cooperate with the House impeachment inquiry. True or false?

29. About what witness called before the Judiciary Committee did Rep. Caldwell Butler say: "He seems to be trying to be candid, but he hasn't had much experience in that area"?
    a) Colson
    b) Magruder
    c) Harmony

30. How did Chairman Peter Rodino respond to White House charges that members of the Judiciary Committee who leaked evidence to the press were "nameless, faceless character assassins" and that they were "a clique of Nixon-hating partisans" engaged in "a purposeful effort to bring down the President," and also that Rodino had personally "not demonstrated any enthusiasm for running down the weasels in his own hen house"?
    a) He ignored it.
    b) He excoriated the White House for cheap-shot tactics.
    c) He said he would do his job.

31. What did Ken Clawson, White House communications director, assert was the true purpose of the Judiciary Committee's writing confidential memoranda?
    a) "Trial preparation"
    b) "Setting up the President's impeachment"
    c) "Slandering President Nixon"

32. Who did two Judiciary Committee congressmen feel "personifie[d] the stonewall" and from whom getting information was "like trying to nail a drop of water to the wall"?
    a) Mitchell
    b) Dean
    c) Nixon

33. During June 1974, the author asked a lawyer for the Republican staff of the House Judiciary Committee how he was able to help present a defense of the President. Guess the response.
    a) "No problem—just ignore nine-tenths of the evidence."
    b) "Why pursue it with you? You never gave Nixon a break anyway."
    c) "I'd love to discuss this with you, but it would be wrong, that's for sure."

34. Just before the Judiciary Committee impeachment debate, Nixon tried to get Alabama Governor George Wallace to use his influence with wavering Alabama Congressman Walter Flowers. When Wallace refused, what did Nixon say to Haig?
    a) "He didn't have to say that. It was deliberate."
    b) "There goes the presidency."
    c) "Where's Colson when you really need him?"

35. After the impeachment vote in the House Judiciary Committee, what did the sergeant-at-arms tell Chairman Peter Rodino?
    a) He supported the vote but felt no joy in it.
    b) A kamikaze pilot had just taken off from National Airport and was heading for the committee chamber.
    c) It was a sad day for the country, and the chairman would surely regret it.

36. Nixon was the first President to be served a subpoena. True or false?

37. What did Nixon state must be "definitive"?

38. What was the significance of Justice Stewart's asking Jaworski at oral argument: "[A]s a matter of law, [Nixon's] position is that he is the sole judge [of what is privileged under the Executive Privilege Doctrine]. And he is asking the Court to agree with that position as a matter of constitutional law"?

39. Nixon argued before the Supreme Court that the courts of the United States could never examine private communications of the President if he claimed executive privilege. True or false?

40. What version of the closing remark of a then-famous TV show was printed on a bumper sticker displayed on the Special Prosecutor's briefcase that contained the report to the House Judiciary Committee?

41. What did the "smoking gun" tape of June 23, 1972, reveal?

42. After the release of the "smoking gun" tape, what kind of speech did Rep. Charles Wiggins, a Nixon supporter, think Nixon had better have in his pocket if he wanted to survive?

25.

26.

27.

28.

29.

30.

31.

32.

33.

Photo I.D. Quiz #4

43. On the "smoking gun" tape, what did Nixon say about the devaluation of Italian currency?
    a) "The best the Italians can do is hope to contain the loss."
    b) "I don't give a shit about the lire."
    c) "The hell with them. I don't remember Maury [Stans] saying any lire were contributed to the campaign."

44. To what was Haldeman referring when he spoke to Haig the day before Nixon's resignation and droned on about "loyalty," "trauma," and "adverse historical effects"?
    a) The unfortunate effects of Watergate
    b) That Haldeman would send Nixon to prison if he didn't get a pardon
    c) The implacability of the press

45. What did Clay Whitehead call the "Buchen project" and Phil Buchen call the "Whitehead project"?
    a) Secret preparations for the Ford transition team
    b) Nixon's resignation speech
    c) A plan for the return to power of Spiro Agnew

46. Senator Goldwater still thought at this point that Nixon could get enough votes in the Senate to survive impeachment. True or false?

47. Upon the release of the "smoking gun" tape, the reaction of the ten Republicans who voted against impeachment in the House Judiciary Committee was to stick by the President. True or false?

Deep Throat Questions
48. What was the "road map"?

49. Who received a letter with the following words from whom: ". . . I respect your decision [to resign], and I also respect the concern for the national interest that led you to conclude that a resolution of the matter this way, rather than through an extended battle in the Courts and the Congress, was advisable in order to prevent a period of national division and uncertainty."

☆ 10 ☆

AFTERMATH AND REFLECTIONS

"Always give your best, never get discouraged, never be petty; always remember others may hate you, but those who hate you don't win unless you hate them, and then you destroy yourself."
—*President Nixon, August 9, 1974*

"Now I don't mind others looking back. . . . Maybe it'll do their own Narcissus complexes some good, and if it does, that doesn't bother me a bit. But as far as my participating with them in it, no way. I'm looking to the future. They can look back."
—*President Nixon, June 3, 1982*

THE TIMES *(1974–The Present)*

The resignation preceded the pardon, the trials, and the recriminations. Later came the memoirs, seething with finger-pointing, speculation, and, of course, conspiracy theorizing. Watergate will go on forever.

All of you who have struggled this far through the quiz may consider yourselves Watergate buffs. You're in good company. Even Nixon recently mused about traitorous Secret Service agents who may have been responsible for the 18½-minute tape gap and "the possibility that we were dealing with a double agent who purposely blew the bugging operation." Everyone has his own theory as to Deep Throat's identity, and we all would love to know where CIA participation began and where it left off.

Not all of the principals have yet presented their versions of the events, and a few who have done so are reappearing in print. Major works by serious investigators are under way, particularly concerning the role of the CIA, the Cuban exile community, and the alleged April 1972 William Haddad–Larry O'Brien phone call warning the DNC chairman about the bugging. Best of all, though, the National Archives is transcribing all the tapes for release in about three years.

I can hardly wait.

QUESTIONS

1. How did William Frates, counsel to Ehrlichman, characterize the tapes in his opening statement to the jury in the cover-up trial?
   a) "The greatest thing that ever happened to John Ehrlichman"
   b) "Probably the sneakiest, vilest backstabbing I have ever encountered"
   c) "Of virtually no importance at all to this case"

2. What was the result of Judge Sirica's suggestion that Haldeman and Ehrlichman have "heart-to-heart talks with Nixon about getting White House files they might need in the cover-up trial"?

3. What was "Wilson's error bag"?

4. How did Judge Sirica and Prosecutor Neal refer to Wilson's well-publicized "error bag"?

5. What did Mitchell's lawyer say to Judge Sirica at the cover-up trial when the other defense lawyers objected to courtroom spectators' laughing during the playing of the tapes?
   a) "Can we cry, Your Honor?"
   b) "Your Honor, there is nothing funny on those tapes."
   c) "Your Honor, this isn't even one of the funny tapes."

6. After the guilty verdict in the cover-up trial, where did Mitchell say he was going to vacation?
   a) San Clemente
   b) A nice quiet cell
   c) The moon

7. Who said, "I'm here having confessed my role in the Watergate case. I can't measure the impact on this Administration or on this nation of Watergate. Whatever the impact, I'm confident that this country can survive its Watergates and its Jeb Magruders"?

8. Jeb Magruder's college ethics professor (who once noted: "You're a nice guy, Jeb, but not yet a good man. You have lots of charm but little inner strength. And if you don't stand for something, you're apt to fall for anything.") later became chaplain at Yale University and counseled students to burn their draft cards. Who was this man, to whom Magruder later compared himself to justify his perjury?

9. Who said, "Someone asked me last week whether people wouldn't say I was hiding behind God to escape from the Watergate. My answer to them was, if someone wants to say that, I'll pray for them"?

10. At the cover-up trial sentencing, Ehrlichman's new counsel proposed that Ehrlichman be given the alternative sentence of serving as legal counsel to six thousand Pueblo Indians. Contrasting the on-the-spot counsel Ehrlichman could provide compared to a big-city law firm, what ironic turn of phrase did counsel use?

11. Who said the following at the sentencing of Colson: "We cannot accept the principle that men in high government office can act in disregard of the rights of even one citizen"?
    a) Judge Sirica
    b) Prosecutor James Neal
    c) Colson

12. None of the appeals of the cover-up trial convictions was successful. True or false?

13. Several years after the resignation, David Frost paid Nixon $600,000 plus 20 percent of the profits for a series of television interviews. Which of the following did Nixon say to Frost during a break in one of the taping sessions?
    a) "Maybe these tapes will get Watergate behind us, and get it behind now."
    b) "I had this much for my vice-presidential papers until the Democrats screwed me."
    c) "Did you do any fornicating this weekend?"

14. Who termed Nixon "the weirdest man ever to live in the White House"?
    a) Nixon's psychiatrist
    b) Haldeman
    c) David Frost

15. Why did Senator Ervin write *The Whole Truth*?

16. Various Watergate-related personalities stated at one time or another that but for one factor, there would have been no Watergate. Match the man with his "but for" factor.

    a) Sam Ervin   1) Martha Mitchell's illness
    b) Nixon   2) J. Edgar Hoover's opposition to the Huston plan, which resulted in the creation of the Plumbers
    c) Tom Huston   3) Forming CREEP instead of using established Republican National Committee machinery to raise campaign contributions

17. Various other personalities and writers have suggested theories behind Watergate. Which one of the following was *not* seriously advanced as an explanation for Watergate?
    a) Nixon was concealing the worst "White House Horror" of all, i.e., that South Vietnamese hard-liners had paid him off to continue the Vietnam War.
    b) During his Florida vacations, Nixon became part of a conspiracy between gangsters and Cubans, which involved Howard Hughes, Bebe Rebozo, and Meyer Lansky. Watergate was the result of a falling-out of the conspiracy.
    c) Watergate is Nixon's punishment for the bad karma resulting from bringing Liddy into the White House.
    d) Former political opponents Jerry Vorhees and Helen Gahagan Douglas used their left-wing connections to get McCord to act as a double agent and sabotage the break-in.
    e) Nixon's guilty conscience, which caused him to be so self-destructive during Watergate, resulted from his childhood murder of his younger brother.

18. Who termed Watergate the "broadest but thinnest scandal in the history of American politics"?
    a) Nixon
    b) Judge Sirica
    c) Archibald Cox

19. Of all Watergate events, bombshells, etc., which one of the following generated the largest volume of telegraph traffic in Western Union history?
    a) The "I am not a crook" speech
    b) The Saturday Night Massacre
    c) Nixon's resignation.

20. Liddy lent his name to a franchise chain of detective companies called Gemstone. True or false?

21. In his memoirs, how does Nixon explain his statement as revealed on the tapes, "I don't give a shit what happens, I want you all to stonewall it, let them plead the Fifth Amendment, cover up or anything else, if it'll save it, save the plan."
    a) Just musing aloud

b) Locker-room talk

c) Changing strategy on Watergate

22. In his memoirs, how does Nixon explain his desire to pay $1 million in hush money to keep the cover-up going?

a) It was his only real alternative under the circumstances.

b) It was a clever way of smoking out the extent of Dean's participation in the cover-up.

c) It was the only way to ensure that the truth would come out.

23. Who wrote the following about the President: "He did a disservice to the nation and to his own party by stubbornly maintaining that position as evidence piled up to the contrary. His error was sheer stubbornness in refusing to admit a mistake. . . . [He] chose to handle the crisis which faced his administration with the outworn rule of thumb 'leave the political skeletons hidden in the closet and keep the door locked' "?

Deep Throat Question

24. Who was Deep Throat?

Answers

Chapter 1. The Plumbers
1. The White House
2. False. Colson so stated publicly on July 6, 1974.
3. a
4. Haldeman is describing Ehrlichman.
5. John Mitchell
6. Henry Kissinger
7. Chuck Colson
8. Herbert Kalmbach
9. Nixon
10. He didn't have one. Even on fishing trips, Rebozo called him "Mr. President."
11. Chuck Colson
12. Bob Haldeman
13. Herb Klein
14. John Mitchell
15. Haldeman and Ehrlichman
16. b
17. d
18. b
19. c
20. True
21. b) "When you've got them by the balls, their hearts and minds will follow." Colson had this epigram mounted on a plaque over the fireplace in his den.
22. c
23. b
24. Hunt and Liddy
25. c) Colson's father. Colson is quoted as having once said, "I will do anything Richard Nixon asks me to—period."

26. An unstructured but uncompromising system run by Haldeman that required written responses to questions or proposed projects by a certain date (usually too soon), which was monitored primarily by a nagging Higby or Strachan, or by others. The continual pestering for written responses often brought hasty action just to satisfy the "tickler."

27. a

28. Nixon's practice of using layers of apparent decision-makers to insulate himself from the implementation and responsibility for a decision.

29. b

30. False. There was such a written list; Colson maintained the list and added names as he deemed appropriate.

31. a) "Incumbency-Responsiveness Program." Two memoranda from White House aide Fred Malek to Haldeman describe a "program for improving departmental responsiveness in support of the President's election," with examples of successful efforts.

32. b) In Nixon's words, "keeping tabs on lots of people who are emerging as less than our friends" and then retaliating after the election. Nixon continued, "I want the most comprehensive notes on all those who tried to do us in. They didn't have to do it. If we had had a very close election and they were playing the other side I would understand this. No—they are doing this quite deliberately, and they are asking for it and they are going to get it. We have not used the power in these first four years, you know. We have never used it. We have not used the Bureau [FBI] and we have not used the Justice Department, but things are going to change now. And they are either going to do it right or go."

33. Each was on a special enemies priority list, identified by Dean and Colson as "persons known to be active in their opposition to the Administration" and against whom Dean and Colson suggested using the "available federal machinery [e.g., grant availability, federal contracts, litigation, prosecution] to best screw them."

34. a

35. George Shultz

36. Hunt and Liddy, who recruited Watergate burglar Bernard Barker, who recruited Frank Sturgis, Eugenio Martinez, Vergilio Gonzalez, Reinaldo Pico, and Felipe De Diego (referred to collectively as "the Cubans").

37. b

38. b

39. b

40. True. Watergate burglar Eugenio Martinez so testified.

41. Dixon was a comedian who flourished because of his striking resemblance to Nixon. Yes, the White House cared. Haldeman requested an undercover investigation of Dixon, which was performed by White House operative John Caulfield.

42. True
43. False. FBI Director J. Edgar Hoover's fierce opposition prevented implementation.
44. No. Huston himself testified that it was not; the White House said it was canceled, but Dean testified he was never so informed, and two months after it was approved, he was told to get it started.
45. False. Section D of the plan presented to Nixon by Huston contains the following language: "Use of this technique is clearly illegal: it amounts to burglary. It is also highly risky and could result in great embarrassment."
46. a) Rep. William S. Moorhead, the author's father
47. a
48. Among other things, the group was set up to "plug leaks" to newsmen of sensitive White House information.
49. b
50. False. Hunt told the committee he was hired to perform ". . . essentially the same kind of work I had performed for the CIA."
51. Hoover would have none of it.
52. a) Roto-Rooters. Room 16 was their office number in the White House. ODESSA was a World War II German veterans organization; Ehrlichman suggested dropping the name as it might cause unnecessary curiosity.
53. a–3; b–4; c–1; d–2
54. d
55. ". . . we go to jail."
56. a
57. a
58. a
59. As set forth in the memorandum, "a covert operation [to] be undertaken to examine all the medical files still held by Ellsberg's psychoanalyst. . . ."
60. a) Hoover never passed up an opportunity to let Nixon know that Hoover ultimately held the high cards. Nixon also may have believed this, but both of the other reasons were the ones he suggested.
61. True
62. a) Ehrlichman asked the CIA to provide Hunt with resources.
63. Cushman realized that if either element had been present (as in fact both were), it would have been illegal for the CIA to assist Hunt.
64. c
65. b
66. Though very thick, the glasses had no effect on the vision of the wearer; the piece of lead was to be worn in a shoe to change the wearer's walking pattern.
67. False. Liddy said he would have used the knife as a weapon if he had to.
68. a

69. a) Nixon: "Goddammit, Bob [Haldeman], haven't we got that capability in place [i.e., the Plumbers]? How many times am I going to have to tell you? Get 'em back."
70. b
71. Firebomb the Brookings Institution and have CREEP agents remove the documents during the resulting confusion.
72. Dress the Cubans up as firemen and be the first to pull up in a late-model fire truck after the alarm was sounded.
73. b
74. True

Deep Throat Question
75. Deep Throat

Chapter 2. CREEP

1. b
2. Haldeman planned it; Nixon reviewed and approved it.
3. a
4. b
5. a
6. b
7. a
8. b
9. Set up more than 550 dummy committees so that a big contributor could give $3,000 to any number of them.
10. All were dummy corporations set up by CREEP to get around the $3,000 gift-tax limit.
11. Stans would write to a corporate officer. The officer would write a letter to each employee, asking him or her to write a check payable to CREEP and send it to the corporate president. (Some corporations even found ways to reimburse the employee from corporate funds.) The president would then send the check to Stans.
12. False. Here is the procedure: (1) A corporate contributor gives the agency a sum of money; (2) the agency gives the corporation an invoice for services rendered, but does nothing; (3) the agency gives the money to CREEP.
13. True, by ten times ($300,000 for Luxembourg versus $30,000 for Finland).
14. CREEP would arrange to have checks given to a designated Mexican attorney who would deposit them in Mexico. He would then withdraw the identical amount from the account in U.S. dollar drafts made to himself, and give the drafts to CREEP. Hence, there was no record of the contributor. This procedure was nicknamed "the Mexican Hat Dance."

15. True
16. c
17. a) Sloan. The others all controlled slush funds: Stans, $1,300,000; Haldeman, $350,000; Kalmbach, $500,000.
18. d
19. c) Clark MacGregor, CREEP chairman, said Liddy used the money to determine what to do "if the crazies make an attack on the President at the convention."
20. False. A letter from the Associated Milk Producers, Inc., dated December 16, 1970, promised Nixon a $2 million contribution in return for curbs on dairy imports. Two weeks after the date of the letter, Nixon imposed quotas on certain dairy products.
21. True, on March 23, 1971.
22. True. Nixon said publicly on January 9, 1974, "There was no mention whatever of campaign contributions [at the meeting with representatives of the dairy industry]."
23. The price of milk (previously frozen under Nixon's wage and price controls) went from $4.65 to $4.95 per hundredweight.
24. Two months after the election, Nixon increased quotas for oil imports from the Virgin Islands, where Hess owned the largest refinery.
25. $1,000,000
26. a–2; c–1
27. $65,000,000. McGovern raised $14,000,000.
28. b) Two months. The man was John Caulfield.
29. a
30. False. Caulfield's proposed plan for political intelligence for the 1972 campaign was budgeted for $511,000; it included electronic surveillance. Mitchell put a hold on it.
31. a
32. False. At the Ervin committee hearings, Ulasewicz testified that it was the easiest. He said, "[W]rite a postal card asking them to mail you all their leaflets. They will put you on their mailing list and you will have everything."
33. d
34. True
35. Gemstone
36. True. They were held at the Attorney General's office in the Justice Department.
37. c
38. b
39. c) "Not realistic." Mitchell told the grand jury the plan would be "unproductive."
40. b

41. "I should have thrown him out the window."
42. For the purpose of gathering possible dirt on Muskie. It has also been suggested that the real reason was to find out what dirt Greenspun may have had on Nixon.
43. ". . . a Howard Hughes plane would be standing by to fly the team directly into a Central American country so that the team would be out of the country before the break-in was discovered."
44. False. Colson staged a dress-rehearsal sabotage event in 1970 against Sen. Joseph Tydings—a Democrat—by arranging for a false story that alleged illegal real-estate dealings.
45. False. The purpose, in the words of Frank Mankiewicz, the chairman of McGovern's campaign, was "not to influence the result of any single primary election, but to create within the Democratic Party such a strong sense of resentment among the candidates, and their followers, as to make unity of the party impossible once a nominee was selected."
46. True. He said so at the Ervin committee hearings.
47. False. Bush directly contradicted Ehrlichman's view in public.
48. That of Xavier Hollander ("The Happy Hooker").
49. False. Ehrlichman had an FBI file on the subject three weeks before it was publicized. Public revelation of Eagleton's prior treatment for mental health problems resulted in presidential candidate McGovern's rescinding his choice of Eagleton as his running mate.
50. By breaking into Bremer's apartment to see if there were (or to plant if there were not) some papers that tied Bremer to the Democrats.
51. True. Meany said to reporters, "You don't think Chuck Colson made that call, do you?"
52. c
53. Nixon himself suggested it.
54. He told the committee that he knew of no supporting evidence.
55. a) To discredit Democrats generally by sticking them with the burden of having caused the Vietnam War, and Edward Kennedy specifically in case he ran for President against Nixon in 1972.
56. a
57. c) A drunken Conein sat on the cushion concealing Hunt's tape recorder and crushed it.
58. a
59. A picture of Teddy Kennedy in bed with someone who was not his wife. The best Colson could ever do was a picture of Teddy Kennedy leaving a Paris nightclub at night in the company of a woman who was not his wife.
60. c
61. Political prankster Dick Tuck. Haldeman attempted to justify Segretti's excesses by claiming that he was hired as a "Dick Tuck for our side."
62. c

63. a) "Ratfucking" (a Trojan Knights Political Club term). The other terms are CIA jargon for this type of activity.

64. e and h

65. A medal from the Massachusetts Safe Driving Committee.

66. c

67. Chapin was hilariously pleased.

68. True

69. b

70. c

71. a

72. c

73. c

74. a–3; b–1; c–1; d–2

75. b

76. b

77. Republican National Chairman

78. This was the name of a Liddy scheme to have a bunch of hippies acting as McGovern supporters barge into McGovern's hotel suite and, in front of television cameras, urinate on national TV. Martinez once stated that the Cubans were paid to urinate and defecate in public to "give the voters a bad impression of people supporting McGovern."

79. He had reservations to stay in the very same suite right after McGovern.

Deep Throat Questions

80. Haldeman decided that the American public perceived the *x* in Nixon unfavorably.

81. a–1; b–4; c–3; d–2; e–7; f–6; g–5; h–8; i–11; j–10; k–9

82. A secret effort involving ITT to raise and distribute political funds secretly. The Town House Committee, which was run from a Georgetown town house, was never legally registered.

83. (1) Andreas told Dahlberg he would contribute $25,000; (2) Dahlberg agreed to pick up the money in Florida; (3) Dahlberg met Andreas on a Florida golf course, and Andreas gave him the check. Dahlberg converted it into a cashier's check issued in his own name; (4) Dahlberg gave the check to Stans; (5) Stans gave the check to Sloan; (6) Sloan gave the check to Liddy; (7) Liddy gave the check to McCord; (8) McCord gave the check to Barker; (9) Barker falsely notarized the check and deposited it in a Miami bank.

84. Less than three months later, Andreas received a Federal Reserve Bank charter that was approved in record time, and for a bank that would not even be ready for two years.

85. The phony name signed at the end of the "Canuck letter," which was written by White House aide Ken Clawson and appeared in the *Manches-*

ter Union Leader on February 24, 1972. The letter read in part, "We went to Ft. Lauderdale to meet Sen. Muskie . . . one of the men asked him what he knew about Blacks and the problem with them— "We didn't have any in Maine, a man with the Senator said. No Blacks, but we have Cannocks [sic]. What did he mean? We ask—Mr. Muskie laughed and said come to New England and see. . . ."

Chapter 3. The Break-in

1. Nixon
2. True. It is reported that former CIA Director Allen Dulles so described McCord.
3. c
4. b) Soon after the arrest, the Supreme Court decided the *Miranda* case, resulting in a dismissal of the charges.
5. a) Hunt won a Guggenheim fellowship for creative writing.
6. True
7. c
8. a, b, *and* c
9. a
10. b) Magruder later testified that he did not regard Liddy's statement "as a specific threat. It was simply Liddy's mannerism."
11. c
12. b
13. c
14. True
15. a–1 or a–3 or a–7 (the CIA gave the Hamilton alias to Hunt, who gave it to McCord); b–4; c–6; d–5; e–3; f–2; g–1; h–1; i–4; j–6; k–8, l–7, m–8 (Fiorini was Sturgis's real name; Manolo was Nixon's valet.)
16. Frank Sturgis
17. Bernard Barker
18. Eugenio Martinez
19. Virgilio Gonzalez. Gonzalez, who was unable to pick the lock, also had difficulty picking the lock during one of the early Watergate break-in attempts. The burglars finally had to use a crowbar to get into Ellsberg's psychiatrist's office.
20. b
21. d
22. a
23. Hunt and Sturgis.
24. False. They got nothing.
25. Felipe De Diego
26. a) Buying identical pairs of pajamas in a Washington shop. They both also participated in the burglary of Daniel Ellsberg's psychiatrist's office, though they did not admit this to the *Herald*.

27. c) Liddy told Hunt that he had learned from government sources that Cuba was financing Democratic candidates, and that the break-in would turn up the proof. (Liddy later wrote that the purpose of the break-in was to find out what derogatory information the Democrats had on the Republicans.)

28. False

29. a

30. a

31. a

32. a

33. c) Three. On May 26, Hunt and Gonzalez spent the whole night hiding from guards. On May 27, Gonzalez couldn't pick the lock. The May 28 break-in was successful after Gonzalez flew to Florida for new lockpicks.

34. The prints showed rubber gloves on the hands holding the documents for photographing.

35. True

36. True. The bug on O'Brien's phone was the one the burglars were sent in to replace on the evening they were caught.

37. a) Maxie. "Menopause Mary" was Hunt's secretary; Sally Harmony was Liddy's.

38. c

39. The cops were plainclothesmen and did not immediately arouse his suspicion

40. Watergate burglar Barker had decided to conserve the batteries in the walkie-talkie, and so had turned it off.

41. Bennett ran Mullen Associates, a CIA cover agency, and was a good friend of Colson's, who kept him informed of Watergate goings-on after the break-in (and perhaps before). Hunt worked for the Mullen agency before Colson hired him to work in the White House. The Mullen agency set up at least seventy-five dummy organizations to help CREEP raise money before the new campaign law became effective on April 7, 1972.

42. b

43. Nixon

44. False. But a "true" response in this instance is also acceptable because there is as yet no hard evidence directly establishing Nixon's prior knowledge of the break-in. However, based on a confidential conversation with an Administration official, this author believes that Mitchell told Nixon of the break-in beforehand.

Deep Throat Questions

45. Sturgis was convicted of running hot cars between the United States and Mexico.

46. McCord's alias, Edward Martin, came from a character in two of Hunt's spy novels. Martinez's alias, Jean Valdes, came from Hunt's novel

Stranger in Town, wherein a woman named Valdes reminded the hero of another woman named Jean.

47. Posing as sales executives, Hunt and the burglars had dinner in a banquet room at the Watergate, then hid, planning to move up to the DNC, but locked themselves in the banquet room and could not get out until they were let out by the Watergate Hotel staff in the morning.

48. Artimé was a well-connected leader of the Cuban exile community. In photos taken at the Orange Bowl in Miami, he can be seen standing behind President and Mrs. Kennedy when the President reaffirmed his commitment to the Cuban community to support anti-Castro operations. Artimé headed the Cuban Defense Committee, which publicly raised funds to take care of the burglars' families and privately funneled hush money from Hunt to the burglars. Just over two years ago, Artimé was found dead of an overdose of radiation.

49. Just after the burglars were caught, Hunt raced up to Baldwin's room (the lookout post in the Howard Johnson's hotel) to get rid of the electronic equipment. Baldwin (who had already been making plans for bugging the Democrats in Florida) yelled this after the fleeing Hunt.

Chapter 4. The Cover-up

1. c
2. True. On June 23, 1972, upon being told by Haldeman of the reason for the break-in, Nixon said, "Thank God it wasn't Colson."
3. True
4. True
5. c
6. True
7. True
8. True
9. Mitchell, on the day after the arrest of the burglars (June 18, 1972).
10. b
11. False. Nixon did, though.
12. Yes. Dean told Liddy two days after the break-in to advise Hunt to leave the country.
13. a–3; b–3 *or* 5; c–1; d–4; e–2
14. c
15. c
16. f
17. b and g
18. Shred them.
19. c
20. Neither. He gave them to Pat Gray, Acting Director of the FBI.
21. a) Hunt's forged cables attempting to implicate President Kennedy in the 1963 assassination of Diem

22. b) He burned it six months later.
23. a
24. Lee R. Pennington, a CIA agent, helped Mrs. McCord dispose of some of her husband's old CIA papers, but imprudently burned a lot of carbon paper, which engulfed the house in thick black smoke.
25. True. Mitchell said of Nixon's reelection that, compared to what was "available on the other side," it was clear that this was "the best thing to do."
26. "The White House Horrors"
27. c
28. In terms of its original goal, the reelection of President Nixon, it was a success.
29. True. He believed Nicaraguan strongman Somoza would keep a place for him on Corn Island in the Caribbean.
30. a
31. Mitchell, two weeks after the break-in.
32. False. His appointment calendar for the three months after his resignation shows that he saw as many campaign officials as in the previous three months.
33. True. Ziegler was never let in on the cover-up by the other conspirators.
34. b
35. b
36. False. Silbert kept Assistant Attorney General Petersen up to date, and Petersen relayed the information to Dean.
37. True. Dean so believed and told Nixon on March 21, 1973, "Because Petersen is a soldier. He kept me informed. He told me when we had problems and the like. He believes in this administration."
38. False. Ehrlichman asked him to allow written statements and he agreed.
39. He refused to answer.
40. True. Petersen told the House Banking and Currency Committee that the Watergate investigation undertaken by the Justice Department was "among the most exhaustive and far-reaching in my twenty-five years in the Justice Department."
41. False. He wrote each member a letter urging them *not* to subpoena witnesses. The chairman of the committee (Rep. Wright Patman of Texas) was one of the first to suggest a cover-up publicly: "A high-level decision has obviously been made to continue a massive cover-up and to do everything possible to hinder a full-scale public airing of the Watergate case."
42. No. Dean sat in on all interviews with White House personnel. CREEP attorneys sat in on interviews with CREEP personnel.
43. a
44. a
45. c
46. b) Nixon thought the CIA could be convinced that such an investigation

would reveal embarrassing facts about the Bay of Pigs (by which Nixon meant Castro's alleged involvement in the Kennedy assassination and the resulting CIA cover-up).

47. b
48. b) That on that particular day, General Walters seemed to have forgotten how he had gotten to be the Deputy Director of the CIA.
49. True. Walters told Gray, and the FBI delayed following up the laundered money in Mexico.
50. False. Walters refused to put the request in writing.
51. False. The CIA did not have a single covert operation under way in Mexico at that time.
52. True. Helms, Walters, and Cushman so agreed, but only on the condition that the White House put the request in writing.
53. True. The White House tape recording of June 23, 1972 (the "smoking gun" tape) shows Nixon directing the manipulation of the CIA.
54. a
55. a) They said they were anticommunists. The Cubans genuinely believed that McGovern was a subversive. Baldwin stated they "were concerned about McGovern and what he would do if elected and all."
56. True. Such an argument was suggested in a memorandum that was submitted to Judge Sirica on January 17, 1973.
57. McCord was convinced that the government would dismiss the case against him rather than reveal the existence of wiretaps.
58. b
59. c
60. Baldwin made a deal with Prosecutor Silbert to reveal what he knew.
61. False. The GAO found violations.
62. c
63. True
64. ". . . if you try to cover it up."
65. Dean. In Nixon's words at a news conference on August 29, 1972, "[W]ithin our own staff, under my direction counsel to the President, Mr. Dean, has conducted a complete investigation of all leads which might involve any present member of the White House staff or anybody in the government. I can say categorically that his investigation indicates that no one in the White House staff, no one in this administration, presently employed, was involved in this very bizarre incident."
66. c
67. To blame the CIA, and get the CIA to tell the FBI to back off the Watergate investigation.
68. Dean asked the CIA to pay bail and salaries of arrested burglars.
69. To blame it all on Liddy, Hunt, and McCord acting on their own.
70. True. In Magruder's words, "Well, there was some discussion about me and I volunteered at one point that maybe I was the guy who ought to

take the heat, because it was going to get to me, and we knew that. And I think it was, there were some takers on that, but basically, the decision was that I was in a position where they knew that I had the authority to either authorize funds or make policy in that committee, that if it got to me, it would go higher, whereas Mr. Liddy, because of his past background it was felt that would be believable that Mr. Liddy was truly the one who did originate it."

71. Haldeman and Ehrlichman planned to blame the burglary on Mitchell. Mitchell refused to take the blame.

72. A plan by Haldeman to blame the cover-up entirely on Dean

73. a

74. b) By circling page 20 of Woodward's daily *New York Times*, and drawing the hands of a clock on the lower corner of the page to indicate the time of the meeting

75. "Katie Graham is going to get her tit caught in a big fat wringer if that's published."

76. False. He said the money was to keep the defendants from talking to the press or the Democrats.

77. False. He justified it on grounds of political expediency: "[I]f you don't deliver it in secret, our heads will be in their laps."

78. True

79. c

80. False. LaRue refused to provide a receipt.

81. a–2; b–3; c–1

82. a–2; b–3; c–1

83. A "warm drop" involved delivery by a live person to a live person; a "cold drop" occurred when the intended recipient just picked up the cash in a predesignated spot.

84. a

85. a

86. a

87. b

88. c

89. "The laundry"

90. "Running around with $75,000 [in a laundry bag] trying to get rid of it."

91. False. In Ulasewicz's words, "Well, Mr. Kalmbach, I will tell you, something here is not kosher. It's definitely not your ball game, Mr. Kalmbach."

92. Ulasewicz used this term because he would never make a move without Kalmbach's say-so, so he spent a lot of time at pay phones calling and waiting for Kalmbach to return his calls.

93. c

94. b

95. a

96. He was going to blow the whistle on the cover-up as much as he could.
97. He probably wanted Caulfield to assume so, but told him not to say so specifically to McCord.
98. b

Deep Throat Questions

99. On June 18, 1972, police searching the burglars' motel rooms found a notebook with a notation "E. H., W. H." with Hunt's White House phone number. The address book belonged to Barker, and also contained the telephone numbers of Manuel Artimé and the Mullen agency. Liddy was soon linked to Barker by telephone records.
100. 1) Liddy—documents related to wiretapping, burglary, and espionage.
    2) Magruder—documents from transcripts of DNC bugging.
    3) Strachan—incriminating documents from Haldeman's file.
    4) Kalmbach—sensitive financial files from his own office.
    5) LaRue—sensitive financial files from his own office.
    6) Porter—sensitive financial files from his own office.
    7) Stans—pre–April 7, 1972, campaign contribution files.
    8) Sloan—pre–April 7, 1972, campaign contribution files.
    9) Gray—politically sensitive documents from Hunt's safe.
    10) Harmony—documents from Liddy's safe.
    11) Nixon—tapes and (probably) Dictabelt.
    12) Haldeman—unknown, but possible.
    13) Ehrlichman—unknown, but possible.
    14) Woods—possible tape erasure.
101. He kept a metal coin changer of the type used by bus drivers.
102. The memorandum would have helped preserve Cover-up Conspiracy Plan Number One (to blame the CIA) by giving the White House a strong defense of legitimate CIA interests and hence no obstruction of justice in using the CIA to stall the FBI investigation. That it stated the opposite of the truth (and what Helms told the prosecutors), was never sent to Walters, and could have been backdated indicates that it might have been created as a bargaining chip in a special Helms or CIA deal with Nixon, which never came off.

Chapter 5. The Cover-up Unravels

1. b
2. Yes. The phrase "one of our boys is off the reservation" meant, specifically in the case of McCord, that McCord was seriously threatening not to follow the plan of keeping quiet.
3. a

4. d) The CIA was involved—in fact, McCord wrote that the CIA was *not* involved.
5. c) After Liddy refused to talk, the prosecutors kept him hidden for several hours, then brought him out of the jury chambers. The press concluded that he had done a lot of talking.
6. a
7. a
8. a
9. False. Nixon appeared to think this was something that would be known to organized crime: "Maybe it takes a gang to do that."
10. True
11. a
12. Nixon
13. b
14. c) Gray told Nixon that all hell would break loose if he was not at the Agency and able to keep the lid on. He also said he was taking the blame for Watergate.
15. c
16. c
17. "Let him hang there. . . . Let him twist slowly, slowly in the wind."
18. a
19. Dita Beard
20. True
21. a
22. a
23. b) CIA Technical Services Division
24. c) Brown. The wig was widely reported to be red, but the author can confirm from personal observation that it is brown.
25. c
26. False. The FBI results showed that the memo had been typed on a typewriter in Dita Beard's office on or about the memo date.
27. a
28. Ehrlichman and Mitchell
29. Mitchell
30. b
31. True
32. b) Forty years, provisional.
33. a) McCord's letter to Sirica announcing participation in Watergate by higher-ups at CREEP and the White House.
34. c
35. b) Pin it on Mitchell (Conspiracy Plan Number Three).
36. Mitchell
37. Martha Mitchell

38. True
39. c
40. "Once the toothpaste is out of the tube, it's going to be very hard to get it back in."
41. c
42. a) Dean; b) Nixon
43. False. Even after he knew that Dean had gone to the prosecutors, Nixon telephoned him on Easter Sunday and said, "You are still my counsel."
44. Sin, redemption, and the need to break away from crooked friends.
45. False. Dean made the statement.
46. Haldeman and Ehrlichman
47. False. The GOP got only $750,000.
48. False. Petersen refused to stop.
49. b
50. John Connally
51. Connally's switching parties.
52. True. Ehrlichman was truly surprised (so he says).
53. False. They were found several days after the dismissal in Ehrlichman's office safe.
54. b) Nixon, April 30, 1973.

Deep Throat Questions

55. Nixon to Attorney General Kleindienst. As part of a deal to get a $400,000 contribution from ITT for the Republican Convention in San Diego, Nixon would see to it that the decision to allow ITT's merger with the Hartford Fire Insurance Company, which had been allowed by the district court after a Justice Department lawsuit, would not be appealed to the court of appeals because experts had told him the district court would be reversed and the merger disallowed as a result.
56. It was an obvious setup to use against Dean as part of Cover-up Conspiracy Plan Number Four, and against Mitchell as long as Cover-up Conspiracy Plan Number Three was viable. It was a very clever plan because such a report would exonerate the President and implicate CREEP, Magruder, and Mitchell. If the truth about the cover-up came out later, the report would be turned on Dean publicly by Haldeman ("We didn't know about the cover-up because we relied on Dean's false report"). In late March and early April, Haldeman and Ehrlichman had not yet given up on Cover-up Conspiracy Plan Number Three, but were preparing a fourth plan in case it was necessary.
57. Cook was a Nixon-appointed chairman of the Securities and Exchange Commission who lasted only ten weeks in the job. Under alleged prodding from CREEP finance chairman Stans, Cook altered the complaint against Vesco in an SEC enforcement proceeding. Adverse congressional reaction resulted in his resignation.

58. Nixon knew that Dean was negotiating with the prosecutors for immunity in return for his testimony; by shutting the door on immunity, he hoped to scare him back into the cover-up.

59. "They make better electronic equipment and they commit suicide when things get rough."

Chapter 6. The Press

1. a
2. b
3. True. He said he didn't. But concerning Watergate coverage, Nixon did say on October 26, 1973, "I have never heard or seen such outrageous, vicious, distorted reporting in twenty-seven years of public life. I am not blaming anyone for that." If you answered "false," you might consider yourself right, too.
4. True
5. b
6. CBS—70 minutes; ABC—41 minutes; NBC—40 minutes.
7. a
8. True, 93 percent.
9. c
10. b
11. True. Ehrlichman instructed Dean to tell Ziegler nothing. Dean suggested to Ziegler that he "hedge, bob, and weave."
12. c
13. c
14. c
15. True. *Washington Post* society reporters were barred.
16. True. In May 1973 he found records of seventeen such wiretaps in Ehrlichman's safe.
17. False. He never released any such information.
18. False, but Liddy did.
19. a
20. Dan Rather. Rather also claimed that Ehrlichman took active steps to get him fired. Ehrlichman denies this.
21. Walter Cronkite
22. Walter Cronkite
23. Yes. The licenses of two stations in Florida were challenged.
24. c) The networks could expect White House retaliation, including action to divest the networks of their wholly-owned VHF TV stations.
25. e

Deep Throat Questions

26. Nixon's first and foremost political mentor, Murray Chotiner.
27. Ms. Patricia O'Leary was a phony name dreamed up by Colson. She was

the supposed leader of an organization that supported Nixon in an ad written by Colson, taken out in *The New York Times*, and paid for by CREEP. The ad was intended to show grass-roots support for Nixon's mining of Haiphong Harbor in May 1972.

Chapter 7. The Saturday Night Massacre

1. a) Senator Edward Kennedy. "The fine hand of the Kennedys is behind this whole hearing. There is no doubt about it. . . ." (February 28, 1973)
2. a) About 1½ million
3. False. He felt it was inconceivable.
4. False. The vote to establish the committee was 77–0.
5. True
6. He announced publicly that he would forbid them to testify.
7. a
8. b
9. c
10. No. But he said it was only an incident of separation of powers and extremely limited.
11. b
12. a–2; b–3; c–1
13. a
14. "A good forgettery."
15. False. He received *testimonial* immunity, which meant that his testimony could not be used against him.
16. Fear of homosexual attacks in prison.
17. False. Dean never mentioned the notebooks he took from Hunt's safe.
18. a
19. No. He said, "That is the suggestion there."
20. "What a *lawyer.*"
21. False. She testified that she told Liddy, "I can keep a secret."
22. "No." Liddy refused to testify before every committee or grand jury, or at any trial.
23. c
24. c
25. a
26. Sen. Lowell Weicker
27. c
28. True. Dean made a statement to the committee about one of his last meetings with Nixon, wherein Nixon asked leading questions that caused Dean to think "the conversation was being taped and that a record was being made to protect himself [Nixon]."
29. True. He welcomed the revelation of the taping system because he believed the tapes would support his version of the cover-up.
30. c) Ehrlichman. Butterfield revealed the existence of the tapes to the Er-

vin committee; Rose Mary Woods always thought that he was a CIA plant.

31. Nixon
32. c) Archibald Cox, but he only recorded a few, never could get the machine to work satisfactorily, and used a beeper in accordance with FCC regulations.
33. False. Colson did. Right after Haldeman resigned, Ken Clawson said to him, "Chuck Colson is blackmailing Nixon. He's got Nixon on the floor. Nixon didn't know that Colson was taping all of his telephone calls with Nixon before and after Watergate happened. He's got on tape just what Nixon said all through the whole Watergate mess."
34. True, on August 22, 1973.
35. c and d
36. Henry Kissinger
37. True. Kevin Phillips and Albert Sindlinger, favorite White House pollsters, released the results of a telephone poll on August 4, 1973, showing just this attitude.
38. False. According to the poll, George McGovern would have won.
39. True. He told him so privately.
40. True. He so promised Richardson on May 22, 1973.
41. Nixon. Dean served on the staff of the National Commission on Reform of the Criminal Laws, which helped draft the statute. Nixon and Mitchell were strong supporters.
42. c
43. b
44. Yes. He threatened a motion for contempt.
45. c
46. False. Stennis was partially deaf.
47. False. Nor was Stennis ever told that there would be a submission to the court and that the transcripts would summarize the tapes, rather than quote them verbatim.
48. False. All three agreed to it.
49. Brezhnev
50. True. In the basement of a house in Arlington belonging to staff attorney George Frampton's grandmother.
51. False. The FBI arrived to prevent documents from leaving the premises.
52. False. He was stunned. Within ten days after the firing, 450,000 telegrams arrived in Washington.
53. a
54. He declared a worldwide alert of all U.S. military forces.

Deep Throat Questions

55. He was referring to the fact that Sam Dash, counsel to the Ervin committee, had originally selected Harold K. Lipset to be chief investigator for

the Watergate Committee. Lipset had pleaded guilty to a violation of New York law involving illegal electronic eavesdropping.
56. "Executive poppycock."
57. "It's like the guy playing piano downstairs in a bawdy house saying he doesn't know what's going on upstairs."
58. Nixon believed that anyone considering assassination would reconsider with Agnew in line for the presidency. Nixon believed the same reasoning would also apply to members of Congress considering his impeachment. Not surprisingly, he was doubly upset at the prospect of Agnew's resignation.
59. If pro-Nixon witnesses were successful in leaving the impression that dirty tricks were usual in campaigns and that the deeds attributable to CREEP were not unusual for either political party.
60. Harry Toulmin was a federal judge against whom a county grand jury in Mississippi had returned a presentment (not quite an indictment, but similar) to the House of Representatives in 1811, thus providing a legal precedent for including Nixon as an unindicted co-conspirator.

Chapter 8. The Tapes
1. True
2. e
3. False. Nixon offered, but the offer was turned down.
4. False. The missing conversations consisted of (1) the June 20, 1972, meeting between Mitchell and Nixon—their first after the arrest of the burglars—and (2) the Nixon-Dean meeting on April 15, 1973, in which the President learned that Dean was cooperating with the prosecution.
5. c
6. False. There was no system. The system designer tried to keep track by sometimes jotting down names on loose pieces of brown grocery-bag-like paper.
7. False. The practice of maintaining presidential logs at the National Archives had been discontinued because it revealed too much about the President's activities. Archivist James Nesbit testified, "I guess the President got tired of being hit with his own bat."
8. False. Thirty-eight seconds were blank on Nixon's June 20, 1972, recollection as well as on numerous other Dictabelt tapes.
9. b
10. False. Haldeman's handwritten notes taken during the conversation reveal it to have been Watergate-related.
11. True. Woods made the denial knowing that there was a gap on the tape. It

was not until the second time she testified a few days later that she acknowledged that she could have caused part of the 18½-minute gap.

12. True. Ziegler called the suggestion "nonsense."

13. Rose Mary Woods's explanation of how she might have caused a portion of the 18½-minute gap by accidentally causing the tape to erase as she stretched to take a phone call.

14. She was unable to do so successfully.

15. b

16. True

17. True

18. a

19. No one ever found "Part 2."

20. False. Haldeman took that tape and several others from the White House in July 1973. Secret Service records also show that Nixon requisitioned the tape along with others and spent twelve hours on June 4, 1973, listening to tapes.

21. a

22. a

23. a

24. False. Two months later he said, "It is entirely possible that Watergate will not be over anytime soon."

25. The near certainty of more Watergate "bombshells."

26. True. "It depends on when I leave."

27. "Operation Candor"

28. Bob Abplanalp (the inventor of the aerosol spray can valve)

29. c

30. UPI's. San Clemente building permit records showed expenditures greater than $100,000.

31. a) Nixon backdated the date on a deed of donation of his vice-presidential papers to get a huge tax deduction.

32. b) "I suppose some wonder how could the Vice President's papers be worth that. Well, I was, shall we say, a rather active Vice President."

33. a–2; b–3; c–1

34. c

35. b) "Are you the boy's mother or his grandmother?" When the man said he was neither one, Nixon slapped the man's face, said, "Of course you're not," and walked off.

36. c

37. "Nixon chose to dibble and dabble and argued on very nebulous grounds like executive privilege and confidentiality when all the American people wanted to know was the truth. . . . I hate to think of the adage *Would you buy a used car from Dick Nixon?* [italics added] But that's what people are asking around the country."

Deep Throat Questions

38. White House ⎰Oval Office
    ⎱"hideaway office" (Executive Office Building)
    Lincoln Room, presidential apartment

    Camp David ⎰Main Office
    ⎱Office in nearby lodge

    Key Biscayne
    Abplanalp house on Grand Cay Island

    San Clemente ⎰In a government building on Coast Guard land nearby
    On the second floor of Spanish-style mansion adjacent to Coast Guard property

    All nine offices had sophisticated communications equipment.

39. As a boy, Nixon worked for six weeks for the Slippery Gulch Rodeo in Prescott, Arizona, barking for a carnival wheel-of-chance game while taking a cut from the illegal poker and dice games going on in the back of the tent.

Chapter 9. The End

1. True. Haig assigned the task to Ken Clawson, who had written the phony "Canuck letter."
2. Yes, Scott was Nixon's patsy.
3. False. Just the opposite: "I ask you what horrors await this nation if he [Nixon] is able to portray himself as a resigned martyr."
4. "I think you were circumcised by your editor."
5. b
6. b
7. The edited transcripts of White House tape recordings.
8. The acquittal of Mitchell and Stans in the Vesco case.
9. John Dean
10. a
11. No. Nixon's promise to do so was as far as he got.
12. False
13. a) "In our judgment it was of dubious relevance."
14. a) On May 13, Ford said that he had read the transcripts and that they showed Nixon to be innocent of any charge.
15. False. Father McLaughlin went public to do just the opposite: "The President acquitted himself throughout these discussions with honor."
16. a
17. False. The transcripts said so, but the true words (as the tapes later showed) were, "That's the kind I want."
18. No
19. False. The White House version omitted this language.
20. False. The White House version did not contain this language.

21. a) "How in the world did we ever get from *The Federalist Papers* to the edited transcripts?"
22. c
23. Nixon
24. Leonard Garment
25. He suggested that Congress should grant a pardon to Nixon in the event that he resigned.
26. Select randomly five or ten of the most wanted tapes and they would be released.
27. Jaworski had privately implied to St. Clair that he might release to the press the information that the Watergate grand jury had named Nixon as an unindicted co-conspirator.
28. False. He said he would cooperate "in any way I consider consistent with my responsibility to the office of the presidency."
29. a
30. c) Rodino responded, "An unfortunate effort to try to divert the committee from pursuing the inquiry based on the evidence. . . . We're going to go forward." (In short, he took a page from Nixon's book in commenting on the unfairness of the attack, and said in effect, "We're going to do our job.")
31. c
32. a
33. a
34. b
35. b
36. False. Jefferson was the first (in 1807), and he also refused to comply. Jefferson refused to go all the way to Richmond to testify in a criminal trial, but said he would do so in Washington.
37. Nixon asserted that a Supreme Court ruling on the release of the tapes and documents must be "definitive" for him to abide by it.
38. Nixon took the position that legally only he could decide what constituted executive privilege. Yet he felt that he should go to the Supreme Court to confirm his belief. Justice Stewart appeared to be pointing out that by appearing before the Court, Nixon seemed to think that he believed that in fact the Supreme Court (not he) was the ultimate arbiter.
39. True, even if the conversations concerned criminal conspiracies in the White House.
40. "Say goodbye, Dick." The traditional ending of the "Laugh-In" TV show was "Say good night, Dick."
41. That Nixon was right in the middle of the cover-up from the beginning; that Haldeman intended to use the CIA; that Mitchell was the origin of the break-in plan; that Nixon might be able to contrive a national security justification; and that investigation of Hunt would uncover a lot of unsavory things (i.e., the "White House Horrors").

42. Another "Checkers speech"
43. b
44. b
45. a
46. False. Goldwater estimated that Nixon had twelve votes, and possibly up to eighteen, but no more.
47. False. They filed a report in the House of Representatives a few days later, saying they were convinced that Nixon had obstructed justice while in the White House.

Deep Throat Questions

48. The Special Prosecutor's index, which accompanied the evidence from the grand jury to the House Judiciary Committee.
49. Spiro Agnew received these words in a letter from Nixon.

Chapter 10. Aftermath and Reflections

1. a
2. Nothing
3. Haldeman's lawyer's frequent reference to a list of supposed legal errors made by Judge Sirica at the cover-up trial, which would cause convictions to be overturned.
4. Judge Sirica called it "Wilson's windbag"; Neal called it a "ferty bag" (a down-home Tennessee term meaning, according to Neal, "where you got two pounds of manure in a one-pound bag").
5. a
6. c
7. Jeb Magruder, before Judge Sirica at his sentencing.
8. William Sloan Coffin.
9. Colson
10. "It is not the same as being *on the reservation.*" (Emphasis added.)
11. c
12. False. Mardian's conviction was overturned and the charges were dropped.
13. c
14. b
15. Because he knew that Nixon's memoirs on Watergate were grossly misleading if not outright false.
16. a–3; b–1; c–2
17. d
18. a
19. b
20. True
21. c

22. c

23. Nixon wrote this about Truman's handling of the Hiss case.

Deep Throat Question

24. Throughout the Watergate scandal, *Washington Post* reporters Woodward and Bernstein seemed to have an uncanny ability to produce penetrating and accurate stories. "Woodward had a source in the Executive Branch who had access to information at CRP [CREEP] as well as the White House. . . . The man's position in the Executive Branch was extremely sensitive." (Woodward and Bernstein, *All the President's Men* [New York, 1974], pp. 73, 75.) The source, "Deep Throat," refused to be quoted or identified even though he supplied much of the information needed to bring the scandal to light.

The following people have been suggested by knowledgeable Watergate aficionados as likely Deep Throats, and all are reasonable answers: Bob Bennett, Alexander Butterfield, Ken Clawson, Mark Felt, Fred Fielding, Leonard Garment, Dave Gergen, Seymour Glanzer, Alexander Haig, Melvin Laird, Charles Lichtenstein, Richard Moore, Henry Petersen, Ray Price, a composite of several Woodward and Bernstein sources, and a total fabrication by Woodward. These candidates are mostly White House aides and law-enforcement officials, except Bob Bennett, whose contacts would have been White House aides (primarily Colson and Hunt).

The chief source for speculation is Woodward's account in *All the President's Men*; therefore, Throat's conversations in that book must be scrutinized for substance, tone, and the timing of the knowledge he revealed to Woodward. From the outset it is important to remember that Woodward is supposed to have disguised Deep Throat to protect his identity. However, because Woodward's account is a historical document, the author feels that while Woodward would have been comfortable misleading snoopy Throat-chasers with a few bogus but insignificant clues (e.g., that Throat is a smoker, that Throat likes Scotch, or that Throat had access to Woodward's home-delivered *New York Times*), he would have tried to preserve Throat's character and the accuracy of the information communicated.

Throat constantly forced Woodward to dig up his own evidence, and insisted on functioning only as a guide. Admittedly this procedure protected Throat's identity, but it also encouraged the development of new evidence. As more evidence accumulated, more new leads to stronger evidence followed. Throat seemed to fear that without evidence beyond the hearsay of an unidentified source, the White House could deny the *Post's* charges and not be pinned down. The result would have been a stalemate. Woodward speculates that "it was equally possible that Deep Throat felt that the effect of one or two big stories, no matter how devastating, could be blunted by the White House" (Woodward p. 270).

Even though he knew, for example, that Colson and Mitchell were guilty,

Throat emphasized that merely exposing their wrongdoing would be ultimately ineffective.

> There isn't anything that would be considered as more than the weakest circumstantial evidence. But there's no doubt either (that both were involved). "Insulation" is the key word to understand why the evidence can't be developed. [p. 271].

Only through a systematic development of a tight case, supported by hard evidence, could the White House veil be pierced.

> A conspiracy like this . . . a conspiracy investigation . . . the rope has to tighten slowly around everyone's neck. You build convincingly from the outer edges in, you get ten times the evidence you need against the Hunts and Liddys. They feel hopelessly finished—they may not talk right away, but the grip is on them. Then you move up and do the same thing at the next level . . . [p. 221].

Throat also believed that until an insider was prepared to expose the entire conspiracy, the White House could manage it:

> Any congressional investigation is going to have a big problem unless they get someone from the inside to crack. Without that, you come up with lots of money and plans for dirty tricks but no first-hand account or detailing of what happened at the top [p. 272].

Once again, note that Throat emphasized the evidence of misdeeds, not just the misdeeds themselves. Few individuals can opine so authoritatively on strategies for penetrating criminal conspiracies. In fact, very few lawyers would be so knowledgeable. To the author (a lawyer himself), these are the words and the modus operandi of an experienced law-enforcement official.

Therefore, non-law-enforcement officials can be eliminated. Also, the author rejects the so-called composite theory and the fabricated-character theory as afterthoughts of frustrated Watergate buffs. The list has now been narrowed to Prosecutor Seymour Glanzer, FBI Deputy Director Mark Felt, and Assistant Attorney General Henry Petersen. It is doubtful that Mark Felt had adequate internal access to the White House, or would have told Woodward that "hiring those two [Hunt and Liddy] was immoral" as Felt himself recently stood trial for performing illegal burglaries for the FBI. Glanzer has been identified as a primary source for *New York Times* reporter Seymour Hersch, and so would not likely have had a similar arrangement with Woodward.

"Deep Throat had access to information from the White House, Justice, the FBI and CRP. What he knew represented an aggregate of hard information flowing in and out of many stations" (pp. 137–38). Henry Petersen, a Justice

Department prosecutor since 1951, conducted the Watergate investigation from the beginning, and had such access. And the pattern of revelations by Throat to Woodward track the information generated by the investigation.

For example, Throat told Woodward on Monday, June 19, 1972, that Hunt was a prime FBI suspect. The burglary had taken place in the early morning hours two nights before, and the next day (Sunday) police had found Barker's address book with Hunt's name and White House phone number among other papers linking Hunt to the burglars. This information would certainly have been available to Petersen by office hours on Monday, June 19, when he could have told Woodward that "Howard Hunt was definitely involved in Watergate" (pp. 75, 26). Who else in Washington do you suspect was aware of this particular information at this time?

Throat's final revelations to Woodward tie in even more closely with Petersen's charge of the Watergate investigation. Until the Special Prosecutor took over in May 1973, Throat kept Woodward up to date on the investigation. On May 16, before the Ervin committee hearings began, Throat gave Woodward a "laundry list" of spicy items (e.g., Liddy's offer to let himself be shot, clemency offers, threats against burglars straying "off the reservation," blackmail, etc.). By this date Petersen had probably reached the zenith of his White House access, functioning even as Nixon's "principal legal advisor" (Ehrlichman, *Witness to Power* [New York, 1982], p. 381n). It is almost as if Throat were cleaning out his desk in anticipation of the end of his ability to provide good information.

After May 16, Woodward writes of no contact with Throat until the first week in November, when Throat tells him of the gaps on the tapes. The firing of Special Prosecutor Cox on October 20 returned the Watergate investigation to the Justice Department under Petersen (and Nixon), where it remained until the first week in November, when the new Special Prosecutor, Leon Jaworski, took over. As leader of the Watergate investigation at this time, Petersen would have been back in a position to learn of the tape gaps. After this information, Throat is never mentioned again.

People have said that Petersen was a dupe, that he sounds on the tapes like Nixon's sucker. Even as late as spring 1973, Dean told the President, "Petersen believes in this Administration."

On the other hand, Richard Ben-Veniste, a rabidly anti-Nixon lawyer on the Special Prosecutor's staff, believed that Petersen would also have resigned if Nixon had told him to fire Cox. More important, when Cox was fired and the Watergate investigation returned to the Justice Department, Ben-Veniste still felt that "we surely were a lot better off with Petersen than with almost anyone else imaginable as a 'supervisor' from the Justice Department." (Ben-Veniste, *Stonewall* [New York, 1977], p. 156.) At this same time, other Justice Department lawyers urged Petersen not to leave the Department because they believed that Petersen would protect them from White House interference. Peter Reint, another task force lawyer, also favored Petersen, and told his colleagues at a tense meeting after the Saturday Night Massacre, "There are two men who haven't lied about Watergate. Gordon Liddy and Henry Petersen" (James Doyle, *Not Above the Law* [New York, 1977], p. 201). If Petersen's own colleagues were able to hold Petersen in this kind of esteem, the author is slow to buy the notion that Petersen was truly the Trickster's stooge.

Imagine the extreme delicacy of Petersen's position. Here was a career bureaucrat (and a Democrat) who achieved success under Bobby Kennedy at the Justice Department, and yet was elevated to the head of the Criminal Division by John Mitchell. Witnessing firsthand the ruthlessness of Nixon's reprisals against his political enemies must have made Petersen very cautious. And then he was stuck with prosecuting the Watergate investigation under Nixon's watchful eye. Naturally, Petersen would have sounded solicitous of his superiors (and they of him). But as he learned the scope of wrongdoing, the stakes were raised. His experience would have told him that Nixon would probably be able to stifle the investigation; Petersen must have suspected that he would lose his position by pushing too hard. And he would have been right. The initial investigation ended in September 1972 with indictments of the burglars only; Cox was canned for pushing too hard.

What is clear is that this was a complicated man in a difficult position. (Ben-Veniste describes him as "reflective"; Woodward describes Throat as "contemplative.") He was also an accomplished bureaucrat who appreciated where power resided in the federal government. Dean describes Petersen as having

> a certain dismantled, harassed look to him. Henry had logged more than twenty years in the Department working his way to the top through persistence and bureaucratic skill. [Dean, *Blind Ambition* (New York, 1976), p. 106]

Woodward writes that in talking with Deep Throat about Nixon's politicizing the federal bureaucracy, he

> sensed the resignation of a man whose fight had been worn out in too many battles. [Woodward, p. 136.]

At the same time, Ehrlichman believed that

> Petersen was a bureaucrat with a cause; I suspect that his objective was always Richard Nixon's ruin. If I were required to make a nomination for "Deep Throat," Henry Petersen would be mine [Ehrlichman, p. 394].

Petersen almost certainly played the game from the start to avoid upsetting the White House, but he must have hated it. He knew enough to doubt that the investigation could force the truth out into the open, but he could not go public with his knowledge. His career would have been finished, and he would have exposed himself to the vindictive wrath of the Nixon Administration. He would have jeopardized potential criminal prosecutions as well. Besides, with more than twenty years' experience prosecuting racketeers and organized-crime figures, Petersen was almost certainly the most qualified man at Justice to conduct the investigation under the circumstances. By operating as Deep Throat, Petersen could publicly develop evidence that Nixon would otherwise bury in the investigation files. By pointing Woodward in the right direction and forcing him to develop the evidence on his own, Petersen could hope for a continuing stream of sound information backing solid press stories over which Nixon would have no control. This was a risky strategy—Woodward had to be careful and quiet—but it must have seemed the only choice.

Answer Key to the Photos

Photo I.D. Quiz #1
1. Frank Sturgis
2. Howard Hunt
3. Eugenio Martinez
4. Bernard Barker
5. Virgilio Gonzalez
6. The Watergate

Photo I.D. Quiz #2
7. Rabbi Baruch Korff
8. Larry Higby
9. John Ehrlichman
10. Richard Moore
11. Bill Timmons
12. Father John McLaughlin
13. Earl Butz
14. Martha Mitchell
15. Egil Krogh

Photo I.D. Quiz #3
16. Herb Klein
17. Rose Mary Woods
18. Chuck Colson
19. Jeb Magruder
20. Bruce Kehrli
21. John Dean
22. James St. Clair
23. Gerald Warren
24. J. Fred Buzhardt

Photo I.D. Quiz #4

25. David Young
26. John Mitchell
27. Fred Malek
28. Ken Clawson
29. Dwight Chapin
30. Robert Odle
31. Don Nixon
32. Len Garment
33. Bob Haldeman

Scoring the Quiz

If you are keeping score, credit true/false, multiple choice, direct-response questions, and photo identifications for two points each. "Deep Throat" questions, purposely as difficult to identify as the Throat itself, are worth five points each. For questions that have multi-part answers, give each part one point, but no more than ten points total for all of them (including multi-part "Deep Throat" questions). No penalty should be assessed for wrong answers, so guess like crazy. Close answers should be resolved in favor of the quiz-taker. There are a total of 602 questions and a possible score of 1,344 points.

Scoring

Fewer than 50 points: If you are over thirty years old, you must have spent the last ten years under a rock, be unable to read, and not own a television set.

50–200 points: You don't remember much, but have probably learned a lot from taking the quiz.

200–500 points: You know your stuff and must have generally followed the press reports, read some Watergate books, and seen some of the televised hearings.

500–1,000 points: You are a true Watergate buff, and extremely knowledgeable, perhaps because you've done some recent research.

1,000–1,200 points: You were an insider, possibly a lawyer on the Special Prosecutor's staff or a White House aide who boned up on Watergate trivia while at Lompoc.

1,200 or more points: You are Deep Throat. Please write to tell me if I guessed your identity correctly.

Chronology

1969

January

Nixon is inaugurated as President.

May

Nixon authorizes illegal "national security" wiretaps on seventeen reporters and high government officials after leaks of information on SALT and the bombing of Cambodia.

August

The Justice Department initiates antitrust proceedings against ITT in connection with an ITT–Hartford Fire Insurance merger.

1970

July

Nixon approves the "Huston plan," which calls for, among other things, the use of illegal methods to gather intelligence on demonstrators and domestic radicals.

December

A dairy-industry group writes a letter promising a $2 million contribution to the 1972 Republican campaign in return for curbs on dairy imports.

Nixon places import quotas on certain dairy products.

1971

January

Herbert Kalmbach, Nixon's personal attorney, begins soliciting illegal corporate contributions.

February

Nixon begins secret taping of all Oval Office conversations.

March

The Agriculture Department announces its decision not to raise milk-price supports.

Shortly after a meeting between Nixon and milk producers, the Agriculture Department announces a milk-price-support increase. Nixon campaign contributions from the dairy industry are forthcoming.

June

The Pentagon Papers are published in *The New York Times* after being leaked by Daniel Ellsberg. Nixon directs the creation of the White House "Plumbers."

An ITT lobbyist writes a memo linking an ITT pledge of $400,000 for the Republican convention in San Diego to favorable settlement of the antitrust case against ITT.

The ITT case is settled favorably for ITT.

September

Donald Segretti begins recruiting Nixon supporters to act as spies and to perform "dirty tricks."

Ellsberg's psychiatric records are burglarized.

December

Liddy begins developing an intelligence plan for the campaign.

1972

January

Mitchell, Dean, Magruder, and Liddy meet to discuss Liddy's proposed $1 million intelligence plan, "Gemstone," which called for spies, chase planes, electronic surveillance, prostitutes, counter-demonstrations, etc.

February

Mitchell, Dean, and Magruder reject a second Liddy intelligence plan, but tell him to continue planning.

March

Mitchell approves Liddy's third plan, which calls for illegal entry into and wiretapping of the DNC's Watergate headquarters.

April

A new disclosure law requiring strict financial reporting of campaign contributions takes effect.

Financier Robert Vesco, under investigation by the SEC for stock fraud, makes a secret $200,000 contribution to the Nixon campaign.

May

A Watergate break-in and wiretapping takes place undetected. Magruder begins supplying Mitchell with copies of information obtained from the wiretaps.

June

Another Watergate break-in occurs and five agents of the Nixon campaign are arrested.

At Nixon's request, White House aides Haldeman and Ehrlichman meet with CIA officials Helms and Walters to discuss limiting the FBI's Watergate investigation.

Acting head of the FBI, L. Patrick Gray III, at a meeting with Dean and Ehrlichman, is given the Hunt documents, which Dean labels "political dynamite."

Nixon's attorney, Herbert Kalmbach, begins funneling secret payments to Watergate conspirators.

August

Attorney General Kleindienst announces that the FBI's investigation of Watergate will be the "most extensive, thorough, and comprehensive" investigation since the inquiry into President Kennedy's assassination.

Nixon claims his administration has been cleared by Dean of complicity in Watergate.

September

A grand jury indicts the Watergate burglars.

October

The Washington Post reports a widespread Republican espionage and sabotage campaign directed against Democrats.

November

Nixon is reelected in a landslide.

December

Gray destroys the Hunt documents he received in June.

1973

January

The trial of the Watergate burglars takes place. Hunt, Barker, Sturgis, Martinez, and Gonzalez plead guilty. Liddy and McCord are convicted.

February

The Senate Watergate Committee is established.

Senate hearings begin on the confirmation of Gray as permanent Director of the FBI.

March

Attorney General Kleindienst testifies he was not pressured to drop the ITT antitrust case.

The "cancer on the presidency" meeting takes place between Dean and Nixon.

Judge Sirica makes public a letter received from McCord, which charges that perjury was committed at the Watergate trial and that defendants were pressured to keep silent.

April

Gray's nomination as FBI Director is withdrawn, and Nixon and Ehrlichman meet Judge Byrne to sound him out for the vacant FBI post.

Dean tells Nixon he has gone to the U.S. Attorney's office to report the Watergate cover-up.

Nixon announces the resignations of Haldeman, Ehrlichman, Dean, and Kleindienst. Nixon nominates Elliot Richardson as Attorney General, giving him the power to appoint a Special Prosecutor.

May

Former Nixon cabinet officers Mitchell and Stans are indicted in connection with the Vesco contribution.

Judge Byrne dismisses all charges against Daniel Ellsberg, citing government misconduct.

The Senate Watergate Committee begins televised public hearings.

Richardson names Archibald Cox as Special Prosecutor.

June

Challenging Nixon, Dean testifies that the President was aware of the cover-up as early as September 1972.

July

Surprise witness Alexander Butterfield discloses the existence of Oval Office tapes.

The Senate Watergate Committee requests access to certain White House tapes.

The Special Prosecutor asks for the White House tapes.

Claiming "executive privilege," Nixon refuses to release the White House tapes. The Senate Watergate Committee decides to subpoena the tapes, and Cox announces that he too will seek subpoenas.

August

Judge Sirica issues a court order to release nine presidential tapes.

September

Krogh, Liddy, Young, and Ehrlichman are indicted in connection with the Plumbers' break-in at the office of Ellsberg's psychiatrist.

October

Vice President Agnew resigns after pleading *nolo contendere* to income-tax evasion.

U.S. Court of Appeals upholds Judge Sirica's order for White House tapes.

Seeking resolution of the tapes controversy, the White House makes the "Stennis compromise" offer.

The Saturday Night Massacre: Nixon orders the firing of Special Prosecutor Cox. Attorney General Richardson and Deputy Attorney General Ruckelshaus resign rather than carry out Nixon's order. Cox is ultimately fired by Solicitor General Robert Bork.

Yielding to public pressure, Nixon agrees to hand over the tapes.

The House Judiciary Committee begins its impeachment inquiry.

Nixon's lawyers report to Judge Sirica that White House tapes of two key presidential conversations do not exist.

November

Leon Jaworski is named as Special Prosecutor, replacing Cox.

In response to newsmen's questions about his personal finances, Nixon declares, "I am not a crook."

The White House reveals a gap of 18½ minutes in the tape of the crucial June 20, 1972, conversation between Nixon and Haldeman.

Nixon's secretary, Rose Mary Woods, says that she may have caused the tape gap by inadvertently leaving her foot on the control pedal.

December

Congress confirms Gerald Ford as Vice President.

Nixon releases his tax returns for 1969–1972, raising questions about the validity of a $576,000 deduction taken for the donation of Nixon's vice-presidential papers to the National Archives.

1974

January

Electronics experts conclude that the 18½-minute tape gap could not have been caused accidentally.

February

Special Prosecutor Leon Jaworski reports the refusal of the White House to comply with his request for tapes and documents relating to his investigation.

Nixon declares at a press conference, "I do not expect to be impeached."

March

The Watergate grand jury gives Judge Sirica a sealed report believed to deal with Nixon's involvement in the Watergate cover-up.

The grand jury indicts seven of Nixon's former aides for participation in the cover-up.

April

The Judiciary Committee votes 33–3 to subpoena tapes and records of more than forty presidential conversations.

Nixon agrees to turn over to the Judiciary Committee edited transcripts of some of the subpoenaed Watergate tape recordings, "blemishes and all."

May

The Judiciary Committee rejects Nixon's offer of edited transcripts in lieu of actual tapes, and writes that he has "failed to comply with the committee's subpoena."

Jaworski appeals directly to the Supreme Court to rule on his subpoena for sixty-four presidential conversations. The Supreme Court agrees to decide whether the President has the right to withhold evidence of possible crimes from Jaworski.

June

Judge Sirica lifts the order that has kept secret the court papers describing Nixon as an unindicted co-conspirator in the cover-up case.

St. Clair begins his rebuttal before the House Judiciary Committee, contending that Nixon had no advance knowledge of the break-in or any involvement in the cover-up.

July

St. Clair says the President might, for the sake of the "public interest," defy the Supreme Court.

The Supreme Court rules 8–0 that Nixon must release the tapes to Jaworski. Later that evening, St. Clair announces that Nixon will comply with the ruling.

August

Nixon surrenders tapes of thirteen more conversations of the sixty-four subpoenaed by Jaworski. Judge Sirica sets August 7 as the deadline for surrender of the rest.

The President makes public transcripts of three more tapes, among them the June 23, 1972, conversations with Haldeman (the "smoking gun" tape).

Senator Scott, Senator Goldwater, and Representative Rhodes meet Nixon to tell him "the situation is very gloomy on Capitol Hill."

Nixon resigns.

Dramatis Personae

Aplanalp, Robert—inventor of the aerosol spray-can valve, friend of Nixon

Agnew, Spiro T.—Vice President; resigned after pleading *nolo contendere* to charges of income-tax evasion

Anderson, Jack—syndicated columnist

Andreas, Dwayne—grain executive; made contribution to 1972 Nixon campaign

Baker, Senator Howard H., Jr.—Republican; vice-chairman, Senate Watergate Committee

Baldwin, Alfred—Watergate burglary lookout at Howard Johnson's hotel

Barker, Bernard—Watergate burglar

Beard, Dita—ITT lobbyist; whisked out of Washington by Hunt

Bennett, Robert—head of CIA cover operation that employed Hunt

Bittman, William O.—counsel to Hunt

Buchanan, Patrick J.—special consultant to the President

Bull, Stephen—special assistant to the President

Burger, Warren E.—Chief Justice of the U.S. Supreme Court

Butterfield, Alexander P.—presidential appointments secretary

Buzhardt, J. Fred Jr.—counsel to President Nixon

Byrne, W. Matthew Jr.—judge at Ellsberg trial

Caulfield, John J.—employee of CREEP, investigator and undercover agent

Chapin, Dwight L.—presidential appointments secretary; convicted for making false statements

Chotiner, Murray—political advisor to President Nixon

Clawson, Kenneth W.—director of communications for the White House

Colson, Charles W.—counsel to the President; pled guilty to obstruction of justice

Connally, John B.—Secretary of the Treasury; domestic and foreign affairs advisor to President Nixon

Cox, Archibald—Watergate Special Prosecutor until October 20, 1973

Dahlberg, Kenneth H.—Midwest finance chairman, CREEP

Dash, Samuel—chief counsel, Senate Watergate Committee

Dean, John W. III—counsel to President Nixon; pled guilty to conspiracy to obstruct justice

De Diego, Felipe—indicted for participating in break-in of Ellsberg's psychiatrist's office

Doar, John M.—special counsel, House Judiciary Committee

Ehrlichman, John D.—domestic affairs advisor to President Nixon; convicted for perjury and conspiracy in Plumbers' trial

Ellsberg, Dr. Daniel J.—defendant in the Pentagon Papers case

Ervin, Senator Sam J., Jr.—chairman of the Senate Watergate Committee

Fielding, Fred—assistant to John Dean

Ford, Gerald R.—Vice President until August 9, 1974; became President on that day; former House minority leader

Frates, William S.—counsel to John D. Ehrlichman

Garment, Leonard—assistant to the President

Gonzalez, Virgilio R.—Watergate burglar

Graham, Katherine—publisher, *The Washington Post*

Gray, L. Patrick—acting Director of the FBI

Greenspun, Hank—publisher, the *Las Vegas Sun*

Gregory, Thomas J.—student who conducted espionage for CREEP

Haig, General Alexander M., Jr.—Haldeman's successor as White House chief of staff

Haldeman, H. R.—White House chief of staff

Halperin, Morton I.—member, National Security Council

Harlow, Bryce—White House liaison chief

Harmony, Sally H.—secretary to G. Gordon Liddy

Helms, Richard M.—Director of the CIA

Higby, Lawrence M.—assistant to Haldeman

Hoover, J. Edgar—Director of the FBI until his death in May 1972

Hughes, Howard R.—billionaire

Humphrey, Senator Hubert H.—former Vice President and presidential contender in 1972

Hunt, Dorothy—wife of E. Howard Hunt, Jr., killed in a plane crash Dec. 8, 1972

Hunt, E. Howard, Jr.—former CIA agent and White House consultant; convicted Watergate conspirator; Plumber

Huston, Tom Charles—White House aide who designed 1970 intelligence-gathering plan

Inouye, Senator Daniel K.—member, Senate Watergate Committee

Jackson, Senator Henry M.—Democratic senator from Washington

Jaworski, Leon—Cox's successor as Watergate Special Prosecutor

Kalmbach, Herbert W.—counsel to President Nixon; pled guilty to trading federal jobs (i.e., ambassadorships) for campaign contributions

Kennedy, Senator Edward M.—Democratic senator from Massachusetts

Kissinger, Henry A.—presidential advisor on national security; Secretary of State

Klein, Herbert G.—White House communications director

Kleindienst, Richard G.—U.S. Attorney General; pled guilty to failing to testify fully before the Senate

Korff, Rabbi Baruch—chairman of the National Citizens' Committee for Fairness to the Presidency

Krogh, Egil, Jr.—assistant to John D. Ehrlichman; pled guilty to violating rights in the "Plumbers" case; Plumber

LaRue, Frederick C.—assistant to Mitchell at CREEP

Liddy, G. Gordon—counsel to CREEP; staff member of Finance Committee to Re-Elect the President; convicted of conspiracy, burglary, and wiretapping; Plumber

Lipset, Harold K.—first chief investigator, Senate Watergate Committee

MacGregor, Clark—director of CREEP (after Mitchell)

Magruder, Jeb Stuart—deputy director, CREEP; pled guilty to obstruction of justice

Mardian, Robert—deputy manager, CREEP

Martinez, Eugenio R.—Watergate burglar

McCord, James W., Jr.—Watergate burglar; chief of security, CREEP

McGovern, Senator George—1972 Democatic presidential nominee

Mitchell, John N.—Attorney General; director, CREEP

Mitchell, Martha—wife of John Mitchell

Moore, Richard A.—counsel to the President

Muskie, Senator Edmund S.—1972 presidential contender

O'Brien, Lawrence F.—chairman, Democratic National Committee

Odle, Robert C., Jr.—director of administration, CREEP

Ogarrio, Manuel—Mexican lawyer

Oliver, R. Spencer—executive director, Association of State Democratic Chairmen, Democratic National Committee

Parkinson, Kenneth W.—counsel to CREEP

Patman, Representative Wright—chairman, House Banking and Currency Committee

Pennington, Lee R., Jr.—CIA agent and friend of James McCord

Petersen, Henry E.—Assistant Attorney General; conducted Justice Department's Watergate investigation

Pico, Reinaldo—member of Watergate burglar Barker's team who helped plan break-in at Ellsberg's psychiatrist's office

Porter, Herbert L. (Bart)—scheduling director, CREEP; convicted for lying to the FBI about Segretti

Rebozo, Charles G. (Bebe)—personal friend of President Nixon

Reisner, Robert—assistant to Jeb Stuart Magruder at CREEP

Richardson, Elliot L.—U.S. Attorney General

Rietz, Kenneth S.—chairman, Nixon Youth Campaign, 1972

Rodino, Peter—representative from N.J., who chaired Senate Judiciary Committee

Ruckelshaus, William D.—Deputy Attorney General

St. Clair, James D.—counsel to the President

Saxbe, William B.—U.S. Attorney General (after Richardson); former Republican senator from Ohio

Scott, Senator Hugh R.—minority leader of the Senate

Segretti, Donald H.—former Treasury Department attorney; convicted for conducting political espionage and sabotage against the Democrats

Shultz, George P.—Secretary of the Treasury

Silbert, Earl J.—Assistant U.S. Attorney, original chief prosecutor at the Watergate break-in trial

Sirica, John J.—chief judge, District Court, Washington, D.C.

Sloan, Hugh W., Jr.—treasurer, Finance Committee to Re-Elect the President

Stans, Maurice H.—Secretary of Commerce; chairman, Finance Committee to Re-Elect the President

Stennis, Senator John C.—Democratic senator from Mississippi

Strachan, Gordon C.—assistant to Haldeman

Sturgis, Frank A.—Watergate burglar

Ulasewicz, Anthony T. (Tony)—detective, New York City Police Department; aide to John J. Caulfield

Vesco, Robert L.—fugitive financier who secretly donated $200,000 to Nixon campaign; indicted with Mitchell and Stans

Wallace, George C.—1972 presidential contender until an attempt on his life

Walters, Lt. General Vernon A.—Deputy Director of the CIA

Warren, Gerald C.—White House deputy press secretary

Weicker, Senator Lowell P., Jr.—member, Senate Watergate Committee

Williams, Edward Bennett—counsel to the Democratic party in its Watergate break-in suit; counsel to *The Washington Post*

Wilson, John J.—attorney for Ehrlichman and Haldeman

Woods, Rose Mary—executive assistant and personal secretary to President Nixon

Wright, Charles Alan—special White House legal consultant on Watergate

Young, David R., Jr.—White House aide; Plumber

Ziegler, Ronald L.—White House Press Secretary